Writing Humor

"Having attended Ian Bernard's humor writing workshops,
I can tell you first hand that he is simply the best
teacher of humor writing in America today."

FANNIE FLAGG
From her Foreword

WRITING HUMOR

GIVING A COMEDIC TOUCH
TO ALL FORMS OF WRITING

IAN BERNARD

FOREWORD BY FANNIE FLAGG

CAPRA PRESS
MEMORABLE BOOKS SINCE 1969
SANTA BARBARA

A Robert Bason Book
Published by Capra Press
815 De La Vina Street
Santa Barbara, CA 93101
www.caprapress.com

Capra Press Writers Series
Cover and book design by Frank Goad

Library of Congress Cataloging-in-Publication Data

Bernard, Ian.
Writing humor : giving a comedic touch to all forms of writing / by
Ian Bernard.
p. cm.
"A Robert Bason Book."
ISBN 1-59266-023-1 (Trade paperback)
1. Wit and humor--Authorship. 2. Authorship. I. Title.
PN6149.A88B47 2003
808'.02--dc21

2003005983

Edition: 10 9 8 7 6 5 4 3 2 1

First Edition

To my wife, Penny, who up to this day
thought I was a dentist.

Table of Contents

Foreword

By Fannie Flagg

T HEY SAY THAT HUMOR WRITING IS SERIOUS BUSINESS, and it is, but thank goodness for Ian Bernard! He has just written the definitive textbook on the subject, and it is not only highly informative, but hilarious as well.

They also say that trying to teach students what is funny, what is not, and why…is like trying to teach the theory of relativity to tree toads.

They, however, whoever they are, are wrong. Having attended Ian Bernard's humor writing workshops, I can tell you first hand that he is simply the best teacher of humor writing in America today. This comprehensive book touches on all forms of humor writing, from novels to sitcoms, and by example, analysis of established writers, and exercises gives the reader an insight into this most difficult kind of writing. Mr. Bernard can't give you a sense of humor, but if you already have one he can sure show you how to use it effectively. So if you are interested in learning humor writing, or if you just want to laugh out loud, read this book

Preface

UNDERTAKERS AND PREACHERS call it levity, but no matter what you call it, there is a way, a technique, to write humor so that even your best friend won't have to lie to you anymore after dutifully reading your pages. My workshop on humor at the Santa Barbara Writer's conference is always filled with serious writers who wonder why their work inspires coma or a stultifying silence in their readers. Most suffer from a myopia that prevents them from recognizing that most of the world isn't really interested in a forty-page description of their beloved parakeet, even though the bird quotes Goethe in High German. The first step is the recognition of the need for some, make that any, hint of humor. This book will show you in a kind and gentle way to recognize the succor of humor, the sweetness of brevity, and the joy of wit. Or maybe that should be the joy of brevity and the sweetness of wit.

Most writers know when they have a problem but are unable to solve it – that is in a way that does no bodily harm. There also seems to be an unwritten law that says the more serious you are, the longer you can go on about it. Erudition can be a heady wine that leads the writer to state his case with endless variations. It's easier to know when you're hurting someone's feelings than when you're boring them. I also discovered the more serious the book, the less the author recognizes the boredom factor. Most of the writers in the workshop do solve the problem and do so without injuring themselves or their work. With the possible exception of Herman Hesse, I can't think of any authors who have not employed a modicum of humor in their writing.

This book will unlock those furrowed brows and present techniques, examples, and insights that will lighten the load and give both friends and strangers fresh incentive to read on and on and on.

What I want to do is make people laugh so they'll see things seriously. –William Zinsser.

The following paragraph is from an article in *Punch*, the now defunct English humor magazine. It was written in the late eighteen hundreds by William Swift:

If humor only meant laughter, you would scarcely feel more interest about a humorous writer than about poor Harlequin.

[The author mentions earlier that Harlequin without his mask was quite a somber person.] *The humorous writer professes to awaken and direct your love, your pity, your kindness; your scorn for untruth, pretension, imposture; your tenderness for the weak, the poor, the oppressed, the unhappy.*

It was evident even then the writer of humor was a very serious person. Then why, you ask, didn't they write serious works instead of humor? I think it best if we leave that question to Freud. You don't have to be funny to write funny. You just have to think funny.

DAVE BARRY'S GREATEST HITS: WHY HUMOR IS FUNNY

Ever since prehistoric times, wise men have tried to understand what makes people laugh. That's why they were called wise men. All the other prehistoric people were out puncturing each other with spears, and the wise men were back in their caves saying: "How about: Here's my wife, please take her right now. No. How about: Would you like to take something? My wife is available. No. How about..." Mankind didn't develop a logical sense of humor until thousands of years later when Aristotle discovered, while shaving, the famous Humor Syllogism, which states, "If A is equal to B, and B is equal to C, then it would not be particularly amusing if the three of them went around poking each other in the eyes and going 'Nyuk nyuk nyuk.' At least I don't think it would be."

There are no guarantees when you write humor. It is

like any other craft. You get better by learning how to get better. This book will teach you techniques and show examples of how to make people smile, so in the future, when they pick up *your* book, *your* play or screenplay, they will keep it in hand for a good while and eagerly turn the page to see what happens next.

I

The Elusive Muse

Men will confess to treason, murder, arson, false teeth, or a wig.
How many of them will own up to a lack of humor?
                                                —Frank Moore Colby

ARE YOU BORN WITH AN INSTINCT FOR HUMOR? Do you subscribe to the Pagliacci theory that your humor disguises the true, depressed, and very serious you? Do people laugh when you sit down to play the piano? How does the writer toiling at the processor know when the material is humorous?

A famous Charles Addams cartoon shows several people seated in a theater facing the stage. All of the people except one are crying. This singular person has a large smile on his face. Without a doubt, this cartoon best describes the predicament of the humor writer. You can tell the same story exactly the same way to two different people. One will laugh and the other will stare at you dumbly. Because there is no scientific definition for a sense of humor, you have to accept the fact that when you commit something to paper, certain people, mostly editors and dentists, will not think it humorous.

But it's a big world and hopefully someone out there will think it funny. The trick is to get some of them to think it funny and, what is even more difficult, persuade them to buy your work.

Humor and comedy are not synonymous. Al Hirshfield, the celebrated caricaturist, said, "Jokes aren't humor. Jokes are easily forgotten, while humor can be memorable. Jokes require a laugh. Humor, while not eschewing the laugh, is satisfied with a touch of recognition or a slight smile."

Roger Rosenblatt, in *The New York Times:*

The humorist knows you are tired, wicked, afraid, frazzled and desperately alone...he is so furious at the world's crookedness, cruelty, shabbiness and cant, that he uses funny material to save himself as well as you.... Humor is character, comedy, personality.

That sense of recognition gives humor a long-lasting effect while jokes are easily forgotten. Comedy is regional in that it encompasses an area where prejudices, dialects, and cultural styles are shared, whereas humor can be universal.

If you write a comedic play and few laugh at the performance, you're a failure. Not so with drama. There are degrees of success and failure with drama. Certain parts may fail, and while they affect the overall success, they don't damn the production outright. Comedy is quite different. If they don't laugh, it's a bomb. But the biggest difference is this: Drama, the world over, draws from the same basic human experience, and there's a similarity from country to country, culture to culture. That's why Shakespeare translates all over the world with great success. But a writer like Neil Simon will not have the same success. He relies on the cultural traits of America to make his comedy work. But to be fair to Mr. Simon, he puts enough humor into his scripts that it doesn't matter if they get all the jokes. What is evident though is this: humor changes from country to country and even from region to region except for one category – broad physical comedy. The guy slipping on the banana peel will get a laugh anywhere.

H.L. Mencken said, "There are no dull subjects. There are only dull writers." If you're attempting to write humor it is important to assume he was right. Humor and comedy wear many different hats and sometimes the hats fit each category. So it follows: If the rules are loosely defined, it makes the game that much harder. The following is a list of some types of comedy and humor. You'll soon realize the lines between them are quite thin.

Farce: Where comic action is central. The jokes are broad, the characters stereotypical. This style is usually found in plays and movies. Plays by Moliere, movies by Laurel and Hardy, Jerry Lewis, Mel Brooks.

Vaudeville and Burlesque: The forerunners of today's sitcoms. Consist of short comedy sketches, songs, and one-liners. The stand-up comedian is a modern-day example, as are TV shows like "Saturday Night Live" and "Laugh In."

Parody: A strong literary device where a serious subject is imitated in a sarcastic fashion. Most of the time the writer imitates the style and subject with obvious exaggeration. Note: You must be aware that the subject you're parodying is not a humorous one, because there is an adage that says "you can't parody parody." "It is not easy to satirize the absurd when the absurd has become official." – S.J. Perelman (interview, 1973)

Satire: Close to parody but the writer usually makes fun of the subject without imitation. Satire utilizes exaggeration, irony and sarcasm: The writer pokes fun at the subject. George S. Kaufman, speaking of New York plays, once said: "Satire is what closes on Saturday night."

Comedy of Manners: This is where wit and sarcasm play an important part. This also encompasses the romantic comedy. See any of the Fred Astaire and Ginger Rogers pictures or *The Philadelphia Story,* screenplay by Donald Ogden Stewart from a play by Philip Barry. *The Importance of Being Ernest,* by Oscar Wilde. The very best sitcoms, like "Cheers," employ comedy of manners.

Realistic Comedy: The serious theme laced with irony and sarcasm. This genre usually includes elements of black humor. *Catch 22* is a great example.

Black Humor: Taboo subjects…death, religion, and sexual oddities handled in a macabre fashion. Arthur Kopit's play *Oh Dad, Poor Dad, Mama's Hung You In The Closet And*

I'm Feeling So Sad is an excellent example. (Screenplay by yours truly.)

Folk and Ethnic Humor: In these politically correct times this may be a dangerous style to attempt. It is imperative the writing be done in a loving way. *Fried Green Tomatoes at the Whistle Stop Café,* by Fannie Flagg.

Wit: The fast come-back, repartee. "She's been in more laps than a napkin." – Mae West. "You can pretend to be serious, but you can't pretend to be witty." – Sacha Guitry. Leo Rosten wrote: "Humor is much broader, more benevolent, more spacious, less acidulous (or nasty) than wit. We smile fondly at humor, which is enduring; but we laugh, often with malice, at wit."

All of these types may intermingle within the writing as long as you maintain a logical style. Joseph Heller in *Catch 22* uses all kinds of humor, from farce to gentle irony, but always maintains a uniform style throughout his writing. Let's say that you don't want to write a comedic novel or short story. That doesn't mean that you can't have a certain amount of humor in your work. So many serious novelists write extremely funny scenes. The characters up to those moments were involved with high drama then all of a sudden became involved with something quite funny. Was this a happy accident on the author's part? I don't believe so. Most good authors realize the importance of humor as a device to allow the reader to breathe. The introduction of humor releases tension and that release allows the drama to build again. Throughout the ages this has been called "comic relief." The fact is most people, with few exceptions, some time or other think something is funny.

It is your job to find those moments!

In the following chapters we'll discuss various techniques that will help you find the ways to include humor in your writing. Please be prepared to accept the fact that nine people may read your stuff without a hint of a grin. But then the tenth person will come along and think you're damn funny. You can be sure the odds will improve as you become more confident.

2
The Human Condition

All humans have one or more of these seven causes: Chance, nature, compulsion, habit, reason, passion, desire. —ARISTOTLE

I'M SURE ARISTOTLE KNEW that with all of those conflicting emotions roiling in the brain, we would not be able to cope if we didn't have a sense of humor. Thankfully, most of us do. Not a day goes by when there isn't some item in the newspaper that illustrates just how funny we all are. In the midst of all the serious news, the tragic accidents, the murders, the natural disasters, a story emerges that, no matter how straight it's written, is simply hilarious. For years I have collected these items and this is my favorite. It appeared in the *Los Angeles Times* around 1994:

SEX SHOW COSTS HOTEL'S KOSHER LICENSE

JERUSALEM – The chief rabbi of Tiberias has revoked the kosher food license of a hotel for allowing a naked couple to have sex in a helicopter hovering above its pool during a New Year's Eve party, the Jerusalem Post said Sunday.

The newspaper said the twenty-minute live aerial sex act, the main attraction of the sold-out party at the Tiberias Club Hotel, was watched by guests from their bedrooms. Chief Rabbi David Perts said the hotel had sinned and did not deserve a license to serve kosher food.

Is it possible to make up such a bizarre tale? Is it not worthy of Fellini? The fact is we have an infinite capacity to rationalize the most extraordinary events as being normal. I'm sure those ordinary people in their hotel rooms in Jerusalem accepted the helicopter sex act couple merely as an unusual show business act done especially for the New Year's Eve party. The next day they went home and talked about it as if they had seen Wayne Newton in Vegas.

The hotel management considered it a sure-fire attraction: much better than a juggling act. You can imagine their discussions about whether or not to have the helicopter hover over the pool or perhaps the outdoor restaurant. But the funniest and most important point to me is the loss of the kosher food license. No civil or criminal prosecution. No moral outcry about pornography. Just this rabbi who considered the act a sin and, as punishment, took away their license to serve kosher food, thus damning the hotel to having only Christian clientele from then on.

You'll notice I left out politics and politicians from the list of daily newspaper happenings. It isn't because they're not funny. The fact is they're too funny. The daily utterances of most politicians have a Kafka-esque tone. The word for it is "spin," which is a euphemism for obscuring the truth. I believe we have become immune to them. Mort Sahl, a brilliant comedian from the '60s, used to read a newspaper and make comments on the political scene. While it was quite funny, the undertone was deadly serious. In more recent times, Bill Maher, of "Politically Incorrect," paid the price for being a bit too anti-establishment. He was canceled. So, if you wish to write political or social satire, do so at your own risk.

What you should look for are the exceptions in common, everyday life, the small items that ring a small bell. The humor writer must learn to be aware of any small and seemingly insignificant moment as that moment may be the key to turning a serious piece into something quite funny. Here is an excerpt from my local paper. The article begins:

JONES, SMITH BETROTHED. [names changed]
David Jones (deceased) and Mary Jones of Santa Maria announce the engagement of their daughter, etc.

Now that's really a good reporter who can talk to the dead.

One of the major airlines put a placard at each seat explaining about the emergency exits on the plane. Here is an excerpt from the placard: *Passengers in exit rows should identify themselves to a crew member if they cannot read, speak, or understand English.*

To coin an expression I truly despise, but in this case is appropriate, "Duh?" I've collected hundreds of these in the past few years and I'll share a few with you. I swear they are all authentic, with no edits or additions.

This is an ad in a mail order catalogue: *Kills Insects For One Full Year With Just One Spray.* It neglects to mention the insects must believe in resurrection.

In the same category, a story headline in the Santa Barbara paper: *Military personnel kill themselves less frequently than civilians.*

A Burger King classified ad in the local paper: *You have the power to shape your future. We are looking for energetic people with great attitudes to join a positive working environment.*

So, if you have lofty ambitions, go to Burger King.

A real estate story in the *Los Angeles Times: I had five kitchens in my other house. In this house we'll have a small kitchen in the study, a small kitchen in the library, a main kitchen and the outdoor one. Mrs. X doesn't cook, but she and her husband like to entertain for charity.*

OK, here's the last one: *6 month old Shih-Tzu to good home, must sell due to allegorie.*

Now if you can't see the humor in any of these items, I'd suggest you ask for a refund.

As you can see, there is a lot of material out there and all you have to do is look at life in a slightly different way. That is you have to allow the wild-and-crazy-guy part of you to emerge. You also have to recognize how the subtleties of language create opportunities for humor. Suicide isn't funny, but military personnel killing themselves less often than civilians is. Humor has a wide range. It can be quite broad or very subtle. It depends on the situation. Do you need a Prussian saber to cut a slice of butter? Writers pretty much utilize the style of humor most like their own. It's easier and, most of the time, so much better.

Humor also acts as a relief valve in very serious situations. There was a segment on a "Mary Tyler Moore Show" called "Chuckles' Funeral," where Mary and the cast attend a funeral for Chuckles the Clown, who was crushed by an elephant during a parade. I might add that Chuckles was dressed as a peanut. Mary begins to picture the incident as the minister drones on about how wonderful a person Chuckles was, and she starts to giggle. She tries to stop – after all it is a funeral service – but cannot. Soon the giggles become audible and she is busted by the minister for laughing out loud. I would label this incident as black humor because of the counterpoint of death with her uncontrollable laughter. It is one of the funniest funeral scenes ever. *Catch 22* is full of moments like that, where death and laughter hold hands.

Smaller moments, moments not so dramatic, can evoke another kind of humor. I call this recognition humor. The reader has shared the experience and sense memory, correlates the experience with what they have just read. Many comedians rely on this kind of humor. Too many perhaps. The typical routine begins: "Have you ever had trouble squeezing the last drop from the tooth paste tube? Or, How about that voice mail stuff?"

The good writer, though, can evoke certain memories common to most people and by so doing, gives the reader a smile. Mark Twain and Will Rogers come to mind as two who could bring the reader into a time and place, then tell the tallest tale and not suspend disbelief. The human condition they elaborated on was so universal we accepted their exaggerations without question. It was our recognition, our past experience, that made the story even funnier. And though each of us is unique in so many ways, there are a lot of behaviors that bind us together. No matter the language, the cultural diversity, or the social category, a lot of Homo sapiens laugh at the same things. Most of the time, those things are non-verbal, but rather simple moments that illuminate the human condition and give a sense of recognition. (Remember the banana peel.)

The following excerpt from Mark Twain takes this very common event, a funeral, and makes a droll comment on it:

AT THE FUNERAL
by Mark Twain

If the odor of flowers is too oppressive for your comfort, remember that they were not brought there for you, and that the person for whom they were brought suffers no inconvenience for their presence....

Listen with as intense an expression of attention as you can command, to the official statement of the character and history of the person in whose honor the entertainment is given; and if these statistics should seem to fail to tally with the facts in places, do not nudge your neighbor, or press your foot upon his toes, or manifest by any other sign, your awareness that taffy is being distributed....

At the moving passages, be moved — but only to the degree of your intimacy with the party in whose honor the entertainment is given. Where a blood relation sobs, an intimate friend should choke up, a distant acquaintance should sigh, a stranger should merely fumble sympathetically with his handkerchief.

Do not bring your dog.

The piece also shows that what we now call "black humor" was popular long before it got its name. You can see that Mark Twain observed the various behaviors at a real funeral and then made humorous comment on them. It is entirely possible that the writers of the "Mary Tyler Moore" segment read this Mark Twain piece. The fact is, a very serious event, such as a funeral, often stimulates a guilty humorous response in people, which they try to suppress. It is therefore quite natural, quite human, material for the humor writer.

So many writers allow their characters to take them on their journey. The characters *speak to them*, and they write it down. Elmore Leonard said that if he creates a character who has nothing to say, he cuts the character out. The fact is your characters must have interesting conversations and compelling inner thoughts or they will be dull. Their interaction with the other characters creates plot and conflict. Too many times writers begin with the plot then cram their characters into it. Ray Bradbury once wrote that the plot is the footprints your characters make through the story. So many times the writer gets a strong idea for a story then finds the characters who serve the idea run out of things to do. While movies can fill out a couple of hours with just an idea (action pictures), writers need characters, and those characters must be strong enough to stimulate the reader's interest from five to five hundred pages.

But the writer must ask: Why are these people in the story? What is unique about them? If the answer is they're just ordinary people living their ordinary lives, then why have you chosen to tell us about them? The fact is they are not ordinary if you have depicted them on paper. That very act sets them apart and the reader has every right to expect something extraordinary about them, no matter how small or trivial. We expect the author to have a point of view. Your characters should have opinions on a great many subjects, even though you don't write them down. What your character thinks reflects on what he does, and those actions tell a great deal of the story.

LAKE WOBEGON DAYS
by Garrison Keillor

Her husband pulls his '66 Chevy into a space between two pickups in front of the clinic. To look at his car, you'd think it was 1966 now, not 1985; it's so new, especially the backseat, which looks as if nobody had ever sat there unless they were gift wrapped. He is coming to see Dr. DeHaven about stomach pains that he thinks could be cancer, which he believes he has a tendency toward. Still, though he may be dying, he takes a minute to get a clean rag out of the trunk, soak it with gasoline, lift the hood and wipe off the engine. He says she runs cooler when she's clean, and it's better if you don't let the dirt get baked on. Nineteen years old, she only has 42000 miles on her, as he will tell you if you admire how new she looks. "Got her in '66. Just 42000 miles on her." It may be odd that a man should be proud of having not gone far, but not so odd in this town.

This is a complete portrait of a man in one paragraph. We know him and all those like him. We also know that in this town, people stay put.

In "serious" writing, the situations are usually dramatic, with dire consequences. Catastrophe, death, drugs, divorce, awful family secrets, and crimes fill each page. With these important themes does the writer want to risk breaking the spell with something less serious: say a bad toothache or an IRS audit?

The answer depends on how the situation is handled. Maybe the rule should be the more serious the book, the less humorous the insertion. But then one should look at *Catch 22*, by Joseph Heller. Here is a book full of war, death, and destruction, and yet it's probably one of the funniest novels ever written. What did Mr. Heller do?

The situations are quite real but are brought to an almost surrealistic level. There is an operatic quality to the book. *Catch 22* has a sense of theatricality. You feel the pain and loss when so many of the characters are killed or wounded, but two pages later you're smiling. There is an absurd paradox at work, and Mr. Heller knew that if he hadn't managed to deftly mix the horrors of war with humor, the novel would have been too hard to take.

Scene after scene in *Catch 22* has a madcap undercurrent of humor while telling the tragic stories of these men caught up in those dangerous times. Mr. Heller clearly had a point of view and strong opinions about the insanity of war. But he knew it would be impossible to tell this in a reportorial style and so he exaggerated the madness and wrote an artistic masterpiece.

CATCH 22
by Joseph Heller

Colonel Cargill, General Peckem's trouble shooter, was a forceful, ruddy man. Before the war he had been an alert, hard-hitting, aggressive marketing executive. He was a very bad marketing executive. Colonel Cargill was so awful a marketing executive that his services were much sought after by firms eager to establish losses for tax purposes. Throughout the civilized world, from Battery Park to Fulton Street, he was known as a dependable man for a fast tax write-off. His prices were high, as failure often did not come easy. He had to start at the top and work his way down, and with sympathetic friends in Washington, losing money was no simple matter. It took months of work and careful misplanning.... He was a self-made man who owed his lack of success to nobody.

A paragraph full of paradox. With the satire on his awful marketing skills, which put him in demand, Heller draws a character who is the antithesis of The American

Dream. He also takes a shot at success, tax planning, and corporate morality. The last sentence is also a very good joke.

Another excerpt:

"Men," Colonel Cargill began in Yossarian's squadron, measuring his pauses carefully. "You're American officers. The officers of no other army in the world can make that statement. Think about it."

The officious character states the obvious with great conviction. This is an ancient comedic device and it works: the unctuous, self-important character who mouths clichés as if they were gems. When you state the obvious, you'd better be sure the words come from a character like that. You also have to be especially careful in writing the narrative in this regard so the reader "gets it." If you're saying something "dumb," make sure the reader knows you know it's so.

One more: Major Major wants to eat with the other officers, but Milo the mess Maitre'd, so to speak, has set him up at his own private table.

"Major Duluth was the squadron commander and he always ate at the same table with the rest of the men."
"It was different with Major Duluth sir."
"In what way was it different with Major Duluth?"
"I wish you wouldn't ask me that sir," said Milo.
"Is it because I look like Henry Fonda?" Major Major mustered the courage to demand.

Once again, Heller leads us into an unexpected payoff.

The Henry Fonda question not only comes from left field, but it also tells us a lot of how Major Major thinks of himself. The fact that he thinks he looks like Henry Fonda tells us a lot about him and thus enhances his character. Throughout the book there are comedic surprises like this, a counterpoint to the seriousness of the war.

The absurdities and paradoxes of life provide ample material for humor. Instead of becoming angry with the phone company for mistakes on your bill, make note of the corporate behavior in response to your complaint. You'll discover there are so many ways for them to apparently agree with you without anything actually being done. We live in an automated world where you can supposedly solve your problems by pushing the correct buttons on your phone. There are so many situations where the machine, the corporate entity, is pitted against the poor individual. What about the waitress who tells you her name and from that moment on ignores your frantic efforts to get her attention? What about the bank teller who agrees the bank lost the records for your deposits and politely tells you that you're overdrawn because of it, but there's nothing to be done about it until the end of the month and you'll still have to pay the fees until it's all straightened out?

What about the police officer who, after you are rear-ended and suffer a large bruise on your forehead, still gives you a ticket for not having your current registration? And what about my experience with the phone company just a while back? They sent me a bill for a phone that was never connected, then refused to cancel the bill because I didn't know the number of the non-existing phone.

You have to train yourself to recognize potential material for humor. You also have to learn how to develop those ideas so they can be inserted into your writing. Here's one more example from my very real life. My ex-wife (to be accurate, one of my ex-wives) and I had a charge account at a large department store chain. A year after the divorce she initiated her own charge account at the store. The store, though, kept sending me her bills. No matter how many times I sent them back with the divorce explanation they continued to send her bills to me. Finally I got in touch with an account supervisor and explained the situation. She then carefully explained to me that the store computer was not set up at that time to recognize a divorce, especially if the people kept the same names: therefore we were still married as far as they were concerned.

A good way to work on this is to take an ordinary situation and ask "what if this happened?" Then ask again and create another scenario. Create as many *what if* scenarios as you can, then choose the best one.

Here is a workplace example from *Something Happened*, by Joseph Heller:

In the office in which I work there are five people of whom I am afraid. Each of these five people is afraid of four people (excluding overlaps), for a total of twenty, and each of these twenty people is afraid of six people, making a total of one hundred and twenty people who are feared by at least one person. Each of these one hundred and twenty people is afraid of the other one hundred and nineteen, and all of these one hundred and forty-five people are afraid of the twelve men at the top....

You can certainly tell from this that Mr. Heller is not going write a serious novel about business. Yet there are no jokes. Just a very odd analysis of a situation by the protagonist. A good idea is to read your passages aloud. You may even wish to record them. Listen to the flow of words. Your ear will tell you so much more than if you merely read them silently.

The writer must look for the paradox, the surprise and the odd turns in the human condition. She must avoid the predictable and straight line of pure logic yet write in a coherent and credible way. Some people call it the suspension of disbelief. When things go wrong it's serious. When things go wrong, then get worse, then more worse (some people would write worser), it's funny.

Here is a basically sad tale told in a very wry fashion. The humor is derived from the passage of time that allows the protagonist to see things in a more philosophical light. The pain is still there, but the sarcastic tone prevails. Even though they are quite obvious, I'll emphasize the words that point out the very funny tone that rescues the piece from being a serious narrative:

I COULD'VE BEEN IN PICTURES
by Linda Stewart-Oaten

A week before my nineteenth birthday, I married my first husband – let's call him "Dick" – at the Little Ivy-Covered Chapel in West Covina. My mother, the official witness and only guest, sobbed through the entire eight-minute ceremony, and when it was over, she stuffed a wad of dollar bills – her tip money – into my bra and raced back to work. Dick's parents, **"unable to** *attend*" (because they had a golf date in Palm Springs), had already given us a **used, 13-inch TV as a consolation prize.**

On our way out, the receptionist, a vision in orange chiffon and cat's eye glasses, handed me a plastic mop bucket and said, "Compliments of the Little Ivy Chapel, Honey." **And that's when it hit me that I was a married woman. Because this wasn't just any old mop bucket. No! This turquoise beauty was brimming with samples of Tide, Rice-a-Roni, Kleenex, Tampax, Del Monte Ketchup, instant Sanka, Bayer Aspirin and a bottle of champagne.**

Of course, it was too early in the marriage for confident predictions, but I thought things seemed to be going pretty darn well. Dick had been polite to Mom and he hadn't started an argument with the rent-a-preacher about evolution or the existence of God. This was so much bigger than just the two of us. We really were, as Dick said, a part of the **"biological imperative." I was flushed with excitement, ready to continue for a lifetime, this sort of heady dialogue.** And then in the parking lot we discovered the car (my car) wouldn't start.

"Damn it, Maggie!" Dick pounded the steering wheel and made his usual angry, implosive, mooing sounds, which I'd come to know so well. "This isn't the fucking battery, is it!? Didn't I tell you to get a new one, like two weeks ago!" **(It was. He did. I didn't).**

Luckily, a middle-aged guy in a Hell's Angels jacket (somebody's best man, as it turned out) overheard our discussion and offered to give us a jump start. We got the motor running and Dick popped the cork on the complimentary bottle of warm champagne and offered the guy a swig.

"Thanks, Son, but I better not," the biker said. "That fizzy stuff just kicks my ass every time." He pulled a silver flask out of his boot, unscrewed the lid and passed it to Dick, who politely took a big gulp. His eyes bulged and he bent forward, gasping and wheezing until he finally managed a strangled "whew!"

The biker laughed. "Good shit, ain't it? My old lady makes it herself." Retrieving the flask, he tilted it to his mouth, swallowed delicately and wiped his lips with the back of his hand. "Care for a taste?" he asked, nodding at me. I shook my head but Dick had guzzled a fair bit of champagne in the interim and was ready for another chug from the flask. And so it went.

By the time we got to my place, I had to ask Mrs. Nagle, who lived in the apartment below mine, to help me get Dick up the stairs.

"So this is him?" she said, unimpressed. **And I must admit, he wasn't at his best, out cold like that and with chunks of puke clinging to his clip-on tie.**

Mrs. Nagle got his ankles as I grabbed him under the armpits, but it was no use, he was just too heavy for us. So the highlight of my wedding night was sitting alone and watching the premiere episode of "Star Trek" on the lousy little TV Dick's parents had given us (which, by the way, had a bad vertical hold), while he slept it off on Mrs. Nagle's kitchen floor next to Rudy, her blind and incontinent poodle.

In case you're wondering, here, in no particular order, are three little words which sum up what first drew me to Dick: handsome, blond, surfer. If you think this makes me sound shallow, you'd be right on the money. But don't forget, I was young and untutored.

Until the wedding, Dick lived at home with **"Ward" and "June,"** his Orange County Uber-Republican parents. Though to give him credit, he'd spent most of his adolescence struggling to distance himself from that whole conservative gestalt. Which reminds me of another reason I was attracted to him: he wrote Marxist love poetry. **At least he said it was his and I had to believe him because it didn't scan all that well. Here, I offer one deathless line from his poem entitled "Forever Red": "I kiss the rough, chapped-knuckle fingers of your righteous worker's hands." Which was followed a stanza or two later by a riff on scrubbing "bourgeois toilets."**

Yes, it's true that in those days his declared goal was to bring Capitalism to its knees, and he gauged the success of each mission by how much it pissed off his parents. His mother, who'd **nearly** been Miss Pasadena and **nearly** made the Olympic swim team, **nearly** O.D.'d on Valium when her boy got arrested at a peace demonstration. Most people who've heard this part of the story say it's **axiomatic that you just don't sell dope to guys wearing black wingtips.** Luckily the charges were dropped when it turned out to be Dick's own special blend of oregano and lawn clippings. But I just know that FBI agent added half a dozen pages to his file out of spite.

Dick's most subversive act occurred June 7, 1965, in the wee hours following his parents' gala twenty-fifth anniversary party, when he impregnated the cleaning lady in the family's kidney-shaped swimming pool.

I happen to know all the gory details about that night because I was the cleaning lady. I'd grown up in

Orange County too – the alternate universe version. My mother was – and still is – a cocktail waitress at Danny Ho's, a faux Hawaiian place near Disneyland. For reasons she keeps to herself, Mom never married and I've never seen my long absent, perhaps even mythical father.

When Dick and I first met, I was cleaning houses for seven different families in three different cities and doing some fill-in waitressing at Danny Ho's. I was trying to save up enough money for cooking school. That was my plan: work a semester, go to school a semester. In fact, I had my whole life pretty much mapped out. Right up through opening my dream restaurant.

Okay, hold on tight because we're going to flash forward three years. Surprise! Against the odds, Dick and I are still married. After mousing around in junior college, he finally got accepted to Berkeley, where he declared a major in engineering (just like his father). Our daughter Skye was by this time two and a half and through some accident of shuffled paperwork, we got bumped to the top of the waiting list and into a WWII-vintage apartment in married student housing. **Not the worst dump in the world but probably a finalist.**

So our marriage wasn't all roses and violin music, but at least now, I thought, we'd finally be safely out of Ward and June's sphere of influence. How could I have guessed that life in Berkeley would so quickly awaken Dick's long dormant Orange County sensibilities? I suspected something was up when I discovered his favorite Ho Chi Minh teeshirt in the garbage. But a week later when he hacked off his ponytail with a rusty Exacto knife and declared that he'd registered to vote as a Republican, I knew the revolution was over. I locked myself in the bathroom and wept because I finally understood that I was married to a man I didn't know. A man who would never again write poetry in praise of my proletarian soul. Skye knocked on the door and said she needed to go potty. **You can't just throw away four months of toilet training so I let her in and vowed silently to make the best of it for her sake.**

With Skye as our emissary, Dick and I quickly got to know Jane and Billy who lived in the building across the court-yard with their four-year-old twins Tinker and Ducky. Initially this was a friendship based almost entirely on proximity and exchanged babysitting.

I think Jane, who called herself a "secular Jew," intimidated Dick a little, with her strident opinions (delivered in rapid-fire Brooklynese, compounded by a sultry smoker's rasp) on subjects ranging from bean sprouts to the proliferation of nuclear arms. She had the thickest glasses and the biggest breasts I've ever seen and an explosion of black ringlets, wound into a messy bun, anchored with well-chewed pencils.

Dick regarded her husband, flabby, pockmarked, slow-talking Billy, with vaguely jocular contempt. But I was touched when Jane told me he'd grown up in a family of snake-handlers in an inbred little holler of Appalachia. Unless you were listening for it you might not even notice the occasional soft twang, because he'd paid for speech therapy to overcome his accent. Billy had escaped the hills with a full scholarship to Harvard, where he promptly had a brief nervous breakdown before meeting Jane, settling in and coasting on a string of gentleman's Cs toward graduation – an asymptote he never quite reached. I gave him extra points for his struggle and for working as a mailman to support

Jane and the twins while she pursued her Masters in Public Policy.

As for me, I was keeping our own pathetic little boat afloat working part time at a tiny macrobiotic restaurant on Telegraph Avenue. The sign over the door said "Burdock and Daikon," but everyone on the Ave. just called it "BAD." **Jane stopped by now and then for a seaweed smoothee.** And if business was slow (which it usually was) we stepped into the alley to have a cigarette. I didn't really smoke but I was test driving a lot of possibilities in those days.

Jane did most of the talking, delivering whole free association soliloquies, whatever was going on in her head at the moment and I have to say, she was brilliant. I was her complement, a great listener. Once I asked if it bothered her that she was so much smarter than Billy. Jane smiled and slowly exhaled smoke through her nostrils. **"Oh..." she purred. "Billyboy has other talents." There was no mistaking her meaning and I suddenly felt so much worse about my own crappy marriage.**

One night, about a month later, I was at Jane and Billy's place to baby-sit Tinker and Ducky when I came across a couple of Polaroids. It's not like I was snooping. They were right there next to the coffee pot, where Billy must have known I'd find them. The first one showed him standing in front of the bedroom closet with a goofy grin on his pock-marked face, clutching his rigid member in both hands, like it was **a Louisville Slugger.** And the other was a profile of Jane. **Without her glasses, her face had a rabbity look. It was a head shot. Well, a giving head shot.** I stared at that one a long time, turning it this way and that, trying to decide if I'd understand what I was seeing if I were just four years old like Tinker and Ducky. I tiptoed to the doorway of *their bedroom and listened to them snore softly, untroubled it seemed by their parents' exhibitionism. Then, I stepped into Billy and Jane's room and flicked on the light. It had an organic, loamy smell, like the inside of an old hat. Clothing and books were piled everywhere. Billy's mailman uniform was tossed over the arm of a lopsided chair. I was surprised to see they shared a narrow single bed. The mattress had a deep hammocky depression in the middle, a nest where their bodies would inevitably roll together and intertwine each night. In the king-sized bed I shared with Dick, there was a carefully maintained no-fire zone in the middle. Okay, I'll say it: my moral indignation gave way to the gnaw of jealousy. I was thinking how Jane's marriage was about passion and mine was about mistaken identities and making the best of it, when I heard their voices at the door. I switched off the light and almost leapt into the living room as Jane and Billy came in, laughing and a little tipsy.*

"How'd it go?" Billy asked.

"Just fine," I mumbled.

"They didn't wake up?" Jane said.

I shook my head and realized I still had the Polaroids in my hand.

"Here," I said and shoved them at her.

Jane glanced at them and murmured, "Uh oh, Billyboy."

"It's really none of my business," I said primly, "but what kind of parents leave this...this kind of...stuff lying around?"

"Ah, now," Billy sighed. "It's not like anybody died. It's just Mama an' Papa lovin' on each other."

"So that makes it okay for Ducky and Tinker to see?"

Billy grinned. "Who d'ya think took the pictures?"

"Oh my God! You are the sickest – "

"Joke!" he said, drowning my fury in a big boozy hug. "Just kiddin' Maggie!" Jane looked on, with a brittle smile as she lit a cigarette and set the Polaroids afire with the lighter.

I waited a second then headed for the door. "Hey Maggie?" he snickered. "Tool like this could save a marriage. You an' Dick ever want to borrow it, just give a hoot."

It wasn't until I was half way down the stairs that I realized the "tool" he was offering was the Polaroid camera. By the time I reached the bottom of the stairs, I decided that from now on, Dick and I would be seeing a lot less of Billy and Jane. And by the time I reached the door of my apartment, I decided my marriage probably wasn't worth saving. Now, eleven years later, Billy and Jane are still married.

The basic story is pretty bleak: a lousy marriage, a joyless, sexless existence with little companionship. If it were told in the present, I think it would be much tougher to make it funny. But the way Ms. Stewart-Oaten wrote it, looking back (I get a sense it was some time ago) and making wry comment, the piece strikes a familiar note, one we can empathize with and enjoy. In fact it is the aura of sadness that enhances the comedic aspects. But Linda is not above writing a good joke, e.g., "It was a head shot. Well, a giving head shot." It pretty much demonstrates that time heals all wounds.

In a later chapter there is a story by James Thurber that is very funny. A husband and wife go to a party after attending a cocktail party where the wife has one too many drinks. The husband is quite embarrassed by her behavior and when it is time to leave Mr. Thurber writes this brief scene:

"I want to lie down," said Mrs. Monroe.

"I'll get your things," said her husband. "Try not to lie down till I get your things."

Hurriedly Mr. Monroe left the room and brought back his wife's coat and handbag.

"My things," said Mrs. Monroe, with bewildering dignity.

The last line, "My things...with bewildering dignity," is a remarkable piece of writing. No, it isn't one bit funny, even though it comes after an extremely funny scene. Thurber changes the mood and we can see the sad, pathetic person in those sparse words. And they are – "my things" and "bewildering."

Exercise: Make a list where your character encounters situations that defy the normal ideas of logic and reason, where innocence is defeated by ignorance and communication is defined by narrow parameters, e.g., 1. Recorded messages at large companies that lead you to other phone messages with every option except speaking to a human being. 2. Employee doublespeak. 3. A rigid company policy. 4. Any uniformed person who tries to fake his way through the conversation.

Give your character different reactions to each situation.

Exercise: In this exercise there is no interaction with anyone else. Your character's inner thoughts describe a situation where life's dirty tricks either run rampant or amble gently. Your character can also make comment on another character's behavior.

> 1. Your character sitting in a restaurant making comments on the diners.
> 2. The Christmas dinner with relatives.
> 3. The work place.

Exercise: Take a dramatic situation from the past and retell it in a humorous way.

A much more difficult situation for the writer is to pick out some tiny incident, some behavioral flaw, and tell it in a manner that inspires our memories and sense of recognition. There are no jokes, no witty dialogue, but simply the warmth and humor of everyday life. The subject itself need not be intrinsically funny. The humor is in the telling. I think the following piece from Shawn McMurray is a good example of this. Look for character and conflict:

7/4 ON DIVISION STREET
by Shawn McMurray

Sit back for a moment and think of the most vivid images you can recall of the 4th of July when you were a kid. Can you see the parade? Maybe it's the flag flying high over the town hall as a brass band played on below. Or maybe it's just a plain old paper plate with a big slice of ice cold watermelon on it. Can you see it? Well if you can, then hug your children and thank the God of your choice because when I think of the 4th of July, I see a limping goat, a raging Korean war veteran and the completely destroyed rear end of a lime green '66 Ford station wagon. Welcome to Independence Day on Division Street. *Welcome to the nightmare.*

[Shawn has tapped into your warm and fuzzy memories of July the Fourth. But then we have the limping goat, the raging Korean veteran, the destroyed '66 Ford station wagon, and the last line: "Welcome to the nightmare," and you know this isn't going be a *Reader's Digest* story.]

The beginning of summer was something everyone on Division Street seemed to look forward to. Our neighbors, the Webers, who had 12 children, looked forward to it because Mr. and Mrs. Weber knew that within a couple of days they would be shipping 10 of them off to Camp Minnetonka for two weeks. The Sanders, our Hungarian neighbors, looked forward to it because the beginning of summer was when the foreign exchange students that Jonosh Sander sponsored each year would show up. They were usually from some unpronounceable Iron Curtain country and were guaranteed the true American experience, which usually turned out to be building Mr. Sander a new patio, resurfacing his driveway or painting one of his friends' houses. And our Chinese neighbors, the Woos looked forward to the beginning of summer because it meant that the 4th of July was just around the corner.

[Pretty straight stuff except for the exchange students Mr. Sander got under false pretenses. A small clue as to what is to follow.]

The Woos were 4th of July junkies. It took them weeks to prepare for what they considered to be the High Holiday of the year. They would string red, white and blue banners over everything that didn't move, bark or bite. They would make sure that each and every one of their lawn chairs was clean and in top working order and they would marinate barnyards full of chicken, ribs and steaks just long enough to insure perfection. When they were sure all the preparation had been handled they would sit back and wait for John Kay to arrive. John Kay was Birdy Woo's brother and it was his job, his only job, to provide the one key ingredient to a really first-rate 4th of July celebration, the fireworks.

[Except for the occasional humorous description, we are still setting the scene and introducing the characters.]

The fireworks laws in Minnesota were pretty clear cut. If you wanted to celebrate Independence Day with anything flashier than a couple of sparklers or a box of caps you were out of luck. That was the bad news. The good news was that Minnesota was right next door to South Dakota, whose pyrotechnic laws were considerable less Draconian. The only flies in the ointment were the state troopers. If they caught you trying to run fireworks across the state border you were probably going to spend the holiday in the jug and be forking over a fine that looked more like a house payment. But if you were clever, could lie in the face of authority, and could stick to your story, you could, in theory, get away with it.

[The beginning of one of the elements of conflict. Like all good fiction, humorous or otherwise, there must be conflict.]

I woke up on the morning of the 4th with the same feeling you get right before you walk into the dentist's office: that feeling of uncertainty mixed with unexplainable terror. My father was busy swearing at the grass in our backyard; my mother was making potato salad and my sister Marsha was halfway through waxing her bike. I made myself some toast and went outside to eat it on our porch. I noticed that John Weber was loading his hoard into his Edsel station wagon and getting ready to go to a picnic at his brother's house. Everyone in our neighborhood was on pins and needles hoping that the Weber's would be gone for the day. In the past, Mr. Weber would begin drinking around 9 AM, and be stinking drunk by noon. He'd then spend the rest of the day screaming at his kids and calling the cops on anyone he figured was having a better time than he was having.

I glanced over at the Sanders' house and saw Bekla and Timori, the foreign exchange students, putting the final touches on the trout pond they had been "encouraged" to build. The two had been in the country for less than a week and had already sided the garage with fake shingles, rebuilt the transmission on Mrs. Sander's Volkswagen and had put in a putting green for Mr. Sander's accountant. They had also, contrary to Mr. Sander's wishes, purchased a suitcase full of fireworks from Danny Woo's private collection. They kept their contraband in the bottom of an antique chest of drawers Mrs. Sander was restoring in the basement. They had unknowingly placed the first piece of the disaster puzzle into place.

[Another piece of foreshadowing. We know something will happen with the fireworks in the drawer. The quotes around "encouraged" to build, point out the author's sarcastic comment.]

I finished my breakfast and decided to go inside and get ready for the day's activities. Getting ready was a simple matter of changing the shorts I had slept in the night before for the shorts I would be sleeping in that night. I brushed my teeth, grabbed my baseball hat and headed out the door.

The Woos' backyard was a study in patriotism. There

were flags everywhere. A cardboard cutout of Mount Rushmore was nailed to the side of their garage next to a banner that read "America #1." Someone, probably Danny, had already drawn a mustache and glasses on Jefferson and buckteeth on Washington. The Woos' dog Scamp was dressed up like a horse. Mr. Woo was busy setting up his barbecue with the help of his eldest son, Earling Jr., and Danny was sitting on the grass reading a comic book. I walked over and sat down next to him.

"What's the plan Dan?" I asked

"Things are running smoothly," he started. "My mom's putting the final touches on her coconut White House cake, my dad is getting ready to incinerate some livestock and my brother David is hunting up some friends for a baseball game. My Uncle John was pulled over by the troopers, though."

The look on my face must have registered the panic I was feeling.

"Don't worry," Danny said. "He had my Aunt Barbara lay down in the back of his station wagon, on top of the fireworks just in case. When the trooper pulled him over, my Uncle told him that she had been bitten by a poisonous spider. When the cop asked him what he was doing in the middle of nowhere instead of at the doctor my uncle told him that they were Jehovah's Witnesses and going to the doctor was a sin. He even asked the cop for an escort to the state line so they could get home quicker for some praying.

[Introduces a comic character who'll soon play a major part. The spider explanation assures us of that. The picture of Aunt Barbara lying down in the back of the wagon is also quite funny.]

I smiled. "That uncle of yours is a national treasure, Danny."

"Amen to that," he said

We stood up and headed towards the house. Danny put his arm around my shoulder.

"Yeah Shawn, we'll play a little ball, eat some burgers and blow shit up. What more could you ask?" I couldn't think of a single thing.

Across the street from the Woos, the Hedlys were getting ready for their 4th of July celebration. Mr. Hedly, his wife, Mary, and their son, Phil, had lived in the neighborhood less than a year. Mr. and Mrs. Hedly were very straight and very religious, and as a result were a real pain in the ass. We couldn't play ball in their yard, we couldn't slide down their hill in the winter and if you swore around them, you were quickly marched home for some good old-fashioned screaming and yelling.

[Like drama, good humor writing relies on conflict. There is also a degree of universal recognition. We have all had a Mr. and Mrs. Hedly in our lives.]

Mr. Hedly was a Korean War veteran who had been shot in the foot for his effort. He walked with a cane, wore a thick-soled black shoe and spent a lot of time reading the Bible and throwing rocks at the Woos' dog Scamp. Even though he was a Christian and spent a great deal of time making sure everyone knew it, he could never really come to terms with his Asian neighbors. To him, a hard working, third-generation Chinese guy was no different than the North Korean sniper that denied him full use of his foot. His wife, Mary, out of respect, shared his views on their neighbors, spent a lot of time working in her garden and *privately drank like a fish.*

As irritating as Mr. Hedly was, he possessed one thing that everyone on our street envied: a pearl white Mustang convertible. Hedly only drove it on weekends, and then only after spending hours washing, waxing and polishing it. The car was Mr. Hedly's alter ego. Behind the wheel he wasn't gimpy old pain in the rear Mr. Hedly, he was the debonair man about town, Chet Hedly. He had a love for that automobile that rivaled or maybe even surpassed the love he felt for his own wife and son. On the 4th of July, he took his prized possession out for a ride, but when he returned, failed to park it back in his garage and opted instead to park it in his driveway.

[Another piece of the disaster puzzle dropped into place. The scene is now complete. Mr. Hedly, the car he loves, and the cast of characters. Something has to go wrong.]

By mid-afternoon things were well on their way. The Kay's arrived, as Danny predicted, shortly after 2 o'clock. We all stood at the top of the Woos' driveway and watched in anticipation as John Kay's lime green station wagon made its way down Division Street, horns blazing. When the car pulled up to the house, we were all a little surprised to see that in addition to his wife and two daughters, Mr. Kay had also brought along a small goat. When pressed, he said that while they were on the last leg of their trip the little goat had run out in front of their car and been hit. He didn't want to just leave the animal in the middle of the road, but didn't want to waste any time looking for the owner either. He wrapped the stricken animal in a checkered tablecloth, tossed it in the back of his wagon and continued on, figuring that

Writing Humor

if it were just hurt, Birdy, who had always been good with ani-
mals, could nurse it back to health, and if it were dead he could
bury it at the Woos'. They took the goat and put it in the garage
with a dish of cold water and went about their business.

[The idea that a dish of water was the extent of their humanitarian effort is quite wry.]

As expected, John Kay had come through as far as the fireworks were concerned. There were explosives for every age range. Tiny red and blue checked Lady Fingers for the children, brick upon brick of Black Cats and Shot Guns for the teens and Cherry Bombs and M-80's for the grown-ups. There were cases of sparklers, bottle rockets and Roman Candles. There was even a box of stubby red stump removers that had no name at all, just an illustration of a Red Chinese soldier blowing his arm off.

[In the midst of all this Americana, the Red Chinese soldier line is a black humor surprise. Shawn is quite casual about it, merely describing the box, which enhances the effect.]

As promised, we played ball, ate like pigs and blew a lot of stuff up. Mr. Woo and his brother-in-law John sampled beverage after beverage as they attended the needs of the barbecue. Their wives chatted, played cards and made sure everyone had whatever they needed. Even Bekla and Timori ventured over after a while for some burgers, lemonade and thick slices of coconut White House cake. It was a fitting celebration of the 190th anniversary of the country's independence.

[The reader is lulled into a sense of calm and may wonder just how far Shawn intends to go. The anticipation is well calculated.]

Across the street, things were considerably more sedate. Mr. Hedly barbecued steaks on his CharmGlo gas grill while his wife busied herself in the kitchen making macaroni salad and secretly drinking vodka and lemonade bracers. Their son, Phil, entertained himself playing catch off the side of the house and wishing he were with us across the street.

Mr. Hedly complained constantly about the noise coming from the Woos and took his anger out on his son by warning him time after time that if he hit the Mustang he would be eternally sorry. They ate in silence as the Woos, Kays and the rest of us carried on like it was our last day on earth.

As it began to darken outside, the more spectacular fireworks were put into play. In the glow of the Tiki torches that the Woos had placed around their yard, Roman Candles were lit and we all watched as the multi-colored spheres shot out like flaming Ping-Pong balls. Waves of bottle rockets were launched into the darkening sky as we wrote our names in mid-air with sparklers. Even the adults put their hands over their ears when John Kay tossed a cherry bomb into the woods behind the Woos home. I laughed until my sides ached.

[The "show, don't tell" action begins and the folksy atmosphere changes.]

I guess it really started when Bekla and Timori decided to go into the Sander's basement to break out their ordnance. They went to the chest, opened up the bottom drawer and were about to remove their stash when Bekla told Timori that he could hold a Lady Finger in his hand while it went off. Timori said prove it. Bekla unwrapped a package of the tiny firecrackers and pulled one from the string and told Timori to light it. The length of time between when Bekla thought he could hold the Lady Finger in his hand and when he realized he couldn't and dropped it back into the drawer couldn't have been more than a second. They slammed the drawer shut and ran to the other side of the room. Shortly after, very shortly after, all hell broke loose. The fireworks all started going off at the same time. The front of the drawer blew off and the rampaging firecrackers were free to roam around, which they did. The two exchange students ran outside and right into the arms of a visibly agitated Jonosh Sander. They all stood at the basement window and watched as 1250 firecrackers did what they do best. When the melee finally ended, Mr. Sander grabbed the two by their shirts and marched them over to the Woos. Someone would have to pay for this.

[The whole preceding paragraph is a great example of painting the picture.]

We had all heard the commotion coming from the Sanders' house but only Danny was laughing. Mr. Sander confronted Mr. Woo as Bekla and Timori looked on wide-eyed. Mr. Sander's rant went from English to Hungarian and back to English again. Meanwhile in the front yard, John Kay was busying himself taping cherry bombs on arrows and firing them into the air. He heard the ruckus, but figured Earling could handle himself and continued on. The shouting match continued until Mr. Sander told Earling Woo to go and clean up the mess in his basement. Mr. Woo was resistant. Mr. Sander marched to the Woos' garage to get a broom. As he opened the door, to his surprise, out shot the quite alive little goat. The animal panicked and ran around to the front of the house right into the legs of John Kay. The timing couldn't have been more perfect. The little goat hit

John at the precise moment he let go of the arrow, which caused it to go off course. As the animal ran off we all watched as the arrow flew into the night sky. There wasn't a psychic among us but as the arrow began to fall we all knew where it was going to land, and it did, right in the front seat of Mr. Hedly's pearl white convertible Mustang. When the cherry bomb blew up, the windshield of the Mustang blew out. Everyone looked at everyone else and it got very quiet. We looked over at the Hedlys' house and saw the lights go on and all of a sudden it wasn't quiet at all. I've never heard anyone swear so loud in my life. Mr. Hedly was using words I still don't know the meaning of. I'd never seen anyone move so fast. He ran up the Woos' driveway like they were giving away free money and without a hint of a limp. There was initially a lot of pointing and yelling. Mr. Woo and his brother-in-law John, who were clearly on the wrong side of the fence on this one, could only stare and take the hit. Jonosh Sander, still holding onto Bekla and Timori, tried to get in on the bashing but both Hedly and Mr. Woo shot him a look that said that his rant would have to wait for another time. Just as it seemed that the Woo/Kay partnership would admit its mistake and make restitution, Mr. Hedly did something I'm sure he still regrets, he called Mr. Woo a stupid Jap. The atmosphere immediately shifted. Not only was Earling Woo not Japanese, being Chinese and all, but he himself had survived over a year in a Japanese prisoner of war camp. He grabbed Mr. Hedly by the shirt and pushed him to the ground. John Kay tried to pull the two apart, but Mr. Hedly had gone crazy. He jumped to his feet and grabbed for the first available weapon, one of the Woo's Tiki torches. He began swinging it in a wide arc. The fuel in the torch began spraying out like dragon's breath. Tiny grass fires were ignited wherever the fuel landed. But it didn't all land on the grass; a small amount made its way into the back of the Kays' station wagon through an open back window. No one saw it at first, and then everyone saw it together. I heard someone yell in slow motion, "Oh my God, no!"

[It is important to note that the damage escalates. Very much like in old movies, there is a flick of whip cream, then another, then one pie, then another until pies are being tossed everywhere. Scenes like these take some careful planning by the writer.]

The wagon began to explode in all points of the compass. Rockets shot out of the windows. Exploding strings of firecrackers danced around the inside of the wagon like a Hades version of American Bandstand, igniting other strings as they came in contact. Birdy Woo yelled, "Someone get a hose!" But when the first of the stump removers went off everyone ran into the Woos' house and down in the basement. Mrs. Hedly saw what was going on from across the street and called in a slurred emergency call to the fire department. In the Woos' basement, everyone's eyes were on Hedly, who tried desperately to find something interesting on the basement ceiling. It was very uncomfortable.

When we heard the wail of the fire engine and then the sound of the firemen putting out the blaze, we ventured back to the surface. John Kay's car wasn't really a car anymore, at least from the driver's seat back. He grabbed Mr. Hedly by his shirt and lifted him off the ground as if he were made of cotton. There wasn't any doubt in anyone's mind that John Kay was about to beat Mr. Hedly stupid and would have if it weren't for the firemen who threatened to wash the two down the driveway with

Ian Bernard

their hoses.

It wasn't long before Officer Eric Olsen, one of our town's two policemen, showed up. He held the two apart as he tried to get the story straight. John Kay yelled over Mr. Hedly while Mr. Hedly yelled over him. Everyone put in his or her two cents' worth. When all the shouting was over, it was Mr. Hedly who ended up in the back of Officer Olsen's prowler. It was a combination of the amount of damage coupled with the fact that Officer Olsen and Earling Woo had been fishing buddies since high school. We all stood in the fog of John Kay's still smoldering station wagon and watched as Mr. Hedly was driven away past his sobbing wife and the shattered remains of his pearl white Mustang convertible.

[The various characters caught up in the multiple disasters give the story a very funny climax. All of the foreshadowing pays off in these vivid descriptions. Now comes the calm after the storm, and we have shared a wonderful memory with the author.]

After a while, Mr. Woo went down to the station and tried to bail his neighbor out, but Hedly wouldn't even see him and ended up spending the night as a guest of the Excelsior Police Department. John Kay, after several gin fizzes, came to terms with his lime green boat anchor and spent the balance of the night singing drinking songs with his brother-in-law Earling while Danny and I spent the rest of the night laughing and chasing his cousins around his yard with Korean sparklers. It was a strange and dangerous day all right and thirty years later I still can't remember having a better time.

Writing Humor

The humor in this piece is based on the universal emotions about the July Fourth holiday. He paints a very normal picture, then, in a subtle way, begins to add characters and action that let the reader know this will not be an actual account of the event. The descriptive phrases, the droll narrative, and the characters make this remembrance humorous. There isn't any witty dialogue nor does the writer step out to make comment. And while it has a great aura of truth about it, I can assure you the writer has skillfully exaggerated the facts to make it more interesting. If this were written in a straight reportorial style, there would be nothing humorous about cars being destroyed, racially motivated fights, and property fires.

The homily goes: The pessimist sees the cup half empty, the optimist sees it half full. The humor writer sees the liquid dribbling down the chin of the fatuous bag of wind trying to act important. The banana peel is there for everyone to slip on. All situations, no matter how serious, have a potential for humor.

George Bernard Shaw said: "When a thing is funny, look for the hidden truth." Will Rogers agreed: "For a gag to be funny, it must be fashioned about some truth." The humor is in the idiosyncratic way of telling.

In 1905 Sigmund Freud wrote a piece called "Jokes and Their Relation to the Unconscious." The piece explained that jokes are a way for us to express thoughts too painful to face. Perhaps the writer of humor observes the human condition too keenly and twists and turns it to make it bearable.

Ian Bernard

Exercise: Write a very ordinary situation involving ordinary people. Then rewrite it introducing a conflict that affects the group, making sure that you exaggerate the events. Choose one of the characters as your narrator, making sure they see the funny side of the picture.

3

The Humorous Main Character

He hasn't a single redeeming vice. –OSCAR WILDE

IN A SOBER AND SANE WORLD there exists a person who, to all outward appearances, behaves pretty much like everyone else. His colleagues at work think he's fine. His family thinks he's fine, and yet you, the reader, suspect that something hidden deep inside him is strange. This hint is subtle. Perhaps just a glance at something or a passing remark. The writer has planted a seed that colors the narrative from that moment on. I know it's perverse, but I always think of the young man who climbs the church steeple and arbitrarily snipes at anything that moves. There's always the neighbor who quotes for the paper: "I don't understand it. He was always such a nice boy."

Of course there was always something there, but it was well hidden. So should it be with your character. You show just enough to upset the psychological applecart – just enough to allow one apple to fall. As the story progresses, one by one the apples tumble down, until at one point the remaining apples all fall out at once.

The dutiful husband, the good father, the CPA is not at all what he seems. The PTA mom who won the state apple pie contest nurtures a secret ambition. How soon you let the apples fall is determined by the nature of your story. When you eke them out slowly your technique is that of a serious writer using a subtle undertone of humor. When you let them tumble out, the chances are you're telling the reader that this is to be a humorous piece. The foibles, habits, behavior, and ideas of your main character perform on the sober and sane page with your "real" characters, and it is the contrast between them that defines just how humorous your main character is, e.g.: A woman sits knitting in a chair, but she has no needles or yarn. Next to her are three other women doing the same action. Not humorous. But this same woman doing the same thing sits at home after a Christmas dinner with the family and nobody pays attention to her. This just might be humorous.

You might say the character in a mainly serious novel may have a sense of humor that he displays whenever it is appropriate. But in a lighter piece of writing the character more often sees things in a humorous way and that defines the style. The writer makes a choice.

I don't mean to suggest that you choose a bizarre action

or behavior to set your character apart. Something as subtle as the inner thoughts making comment can be enough. But in the truly comic novel it doesn't hurt to have a zinger – a line that not only dumps the apples, but crushes them to juice. Take a look at the last line of this paragraph by Christopher Moore in his novel *Practical Demon Keeping*:

Billy Winston was tall, painfully thin, ugly, smelled bad, and had a particular talent for saying the wrong thing in almost any situation. The Breeze suspected that Billy was gay. The idea was reinforced one night when he dropped in on Billy at his job as night clerk at the Rooms-R-Us Motel and found him leafing through a Playgirl magazine. In Breeze's business one got used to running across the skeletons in people's closets. If Billy's skeleton wore women's underwear, it didn't really matter. Homosexuality on Billy was like acne on a leper.

Except for the Rooms-R-Us Motel remark and the skeleton wearing women's underwear, the paragraph reads very straight. Then comes the devastating metaphor. True, it is black humor, but one can't deny it paints a vivid picture. Mr. Moore has presented us with a strange but true fact. Acne on a teenager would not be funny. Homosexuality on Billy, like muscles on Arnold Schwartzenegger, is not funny. Yet they both make sense. You can sure as hell kill a joke by analyzing it but here goes. What does a leper not need the most? Another affliction that affects the appearance? Teenage acne most of the time is transitory. The picture of Arnold with another muscle is redundant.

But Acne on a leper joins humor with pathos and when those two emotions get close, one of them takes over. In this case, it's humor.

Now, having gone through all of that, some of you are saying I didn't think it was funny in the first place. It proves Charles Addams was very astute. Years ago I wrote a play with some dark humor. One night the audience would laugh where I expected them to. The next night they ignored the lines I thought were funny and laughed – according to my mind – in all the wrong places.

Usually the main character doesn't know she's funny. There are no conscious attempts to be funny. Many times, in fact, the character is genuinely surprised by the reactions to her behavior. I'm almost sure that all of you have had an acquaintance or friend who says incredibly funny things without knowing it. Her remarks are also enhanced by her innocence.

When you read a book by an author with a reputation for being humorous, there is an expectation that puts you in the mood to laugh. That expectation begins with the purchase of the book. Hopefully it lasts after you read the first page. It's the same thing when you go to see comediennes perform at a comedy nightclub. By virtue of their past history, certain writers create an aura of good humor.

But when you read an author whose reputation is more as a story teller, whose label and marketing do not stress humor, you lose this expectation, and so when you come across a passage that makes you chuckle, it's a welcome surprise.

The writer should make a choice from page one. You can't start funny and fifty pages later turn serious. But you can begin in a serious tone and interject humor at some point. The problem is if the serious mood you have set becomes so entrenched and you wait two hundred pages to "lighten up," you'll have a hard time changing your tune.

Breakfast At Tiffanys, by Truman Capote, is a perfect example of a funny main character in a well-told story. Holly Golightly doesn't know she's funny. To her mind, her behavior is perfectly natural. The same for *Auntie Mame,* by Patrick Dennis. Both of those characters have a highly individualistic outlook on life that contrasts drastically from the norm. These bigger-than-life characters aren't performing. They simply are what they are. It is the world around them that's out of step. It's important to note that your main character doesn't need to be a wisecracking jokester. It's their different behavior in a normal world that sets them apart and gives a literal meaning to the words "He's a character." Think about when you said that about someone you know. What behavior motivated the description? Then simply transfer those ideas onto a fictional character, making sure you've changed them enough to avoid a lawsuit.

Aldous Huxley, not one of those authors who come to mind when you think of humor, wrote a book called *Antic Hay.* In the book his main character proposes an idea in a very straightforward manner to some very distinguished English gentlemen. His name is Gumbrill Junior and he explains how the idea came to him in chapel during service:

"What are Gumbrill's Patent Small-Clothes?"
"My Patent Small-Clothes may be described as trousers with

a pneumatic seat, inflatable by means of a tube fitted with a valve; the while constructed of stout seamless red rubber, enclosed between two layers of cloth."

"I must say," said Gumbrill Senior on a tone of somewhat grudging approbation, I have heard of worse inventions.... We Gumbrills are all a bony lot."

He explains the invention will be a boon to travelers, concert goers, etc., and he will make a fortune. Here we have an English study, two older gentlemen and the son. The tone is very British, the conversation proper and polite. Gumbrill Junior sincerely believes he has a wonderful idea and Gumbrill Senior accepts it as such. It is only the reader who finds the idea of pneumatic trousers funny. The "serious" discussion of the matter enhances the humor, and of course the description of the trousers completes the job. Throughout the book Huxley uses this droll technique in an understated British manner quite effectively.

Pnin, by Vladimir Nabokov, is another example of a humorous main character who has no idea of his comic effect:

His life was a constant war with insensate objects that fell apart, or attacked him, or refused to function, or viciously got themselves lost as soon as they entered the sphere of his existence....

Nabokov, just before this description, tells us Professor Pnin is on the wrong train. He is a Mr. Magoo, the man who abruptly changes lanes on the highway and drives off leaving ten mangled cars in his wake, then reads about it the paper and thinks that some people don't know how to drive.

PNIN
by Vladimir Nabokov

Now a secret must be imparted. Professor Pnin was on the wrong train. He was unaware of it, and so was the conductor, already threading his way through the train to Pnin's coach. As a matter of fact, Pnin at the moment felt very well satisfied with himself. When inviting him to deliver a Friday-evening lecture at Cremona – some two hundred west of Waindell, Pnin's academic perch since 1945 – the vice president of the Cremona Woman's Club, a Miss Judith Clyde, had advised our friend that the most convenient train left Waindell at 1:52 P.M., reaching Cremona at 4:17; but Pnin – who, like so many Russians, was inordinately fond of everything in the line of timetables, maps, catalogues, collected them, helped himself freely to them with the bracing pleasure of getting something for nothing, and took especial pride in puzzling out schedules for himself – had discovered, after some study, an inconspicuous reference mark against a still more convenient train (Lv. Waindell 2:19 P.M., Ar. Cremona 4:32 P.M.); the mark indicted that Fridays, and Fridays only, the two nineteen stopped at Cremona on its way to a distant and much larger city. Unfortunately for Pnin, his timetable was five years old and in part obsolete.

The main character may be witty, sarcastic, and still not be humorous. Professor Pnin is not a humorous character. But things happen to him because of his behavior, and he suffers through them. In fact it is Pnin's scholastic demeanor that enhances the humor. So when he gets on the wrong train or misses his stop, he is genuinely upset. The problems are real: The reader sees them as funny, while Pnin endures them.

There is an adage in acting regarding comedy that says you don't play the joke, you play the character in the scene. If you apply that to writing, you might interpolate; the character is oblivious to his humorous effect. You'll notice that Nabokov doesn't try to tell the story in a humorous fashion. He lets the facts speak for themselves. But, and this is a huge but, the humor is predicated on the character of Pnin. It is our recognition of Pnin that makes us smile.

Another important aspect of main characters is they must be real enough to be believable. The reader will suspend disbelief at times, but you must be careful not to go too far. Strangely enough, credibility is an important ingredient in humor. When the behavior goes beyond a certain point, the reader gives up and dismisses the story as silly or pointless. Now there is a writing technique that from the start lets the reader know this is to be a nonsense, abstract, bizarre, even avant-garde kind of work and so it is acceptable. There are stories in *The New Yorker* by Steve Martin that employ one or more of these techniques. Woody Allen has also written these kinds of stories. There is little reality and you don't care. I think the father of this kind of writing was S.J. Perelman. The reader simply enjoyed the wildness, the abstraction, for its own worth. But it's important to point out that Mr. Perelman usually had a satiric edge to his work. He took careful aim at some human foible with great style and wit.

For the most part, though, the main character in a work of fiction should have a firm foundation in reality, albeit a fictional one. This allows the writer to create the surprises, the conflicts, and the topsy-turvy that counterpoints the reality.

Our Man In Havana, by Graham Greene, is an example of a main character caught up in a dangerous – but humorous – situation. The hero owns a vacuum cleaner shop in Havana. To make more money he allows himself to be recruited by the English secret service. Now the protagonist is a spy in Cuba for England. He's not a very good spy and in order to save his job he has to come up with something for his bosses. In desperation he sends them the plans for a vacuum cleaner saying they are for some secret weapon. The powers that be in England are very intrigued and the adventure begins. The rest of the novel is based on these plans, which are thought to have important military significance, and the plot complications they inspire.

Here is an excerpt from *High Fidelity*, by Nick Hornby. It is a good example of the first-person main character. The narrator is asked to go see the movie *Howard's End* with his mother and father. His father assures him that seeing the picture will take his mind off things:

And, anyway, he's wrong. Going to the pictures aged thirty-five with your mum and dad and their insane friends does not take your mind off things, I discovered. It very much puts your mind on things. While we're waiting for Yvonne and Brian to purchase the entire contents of the Pick 'n Mix counter, I have a terrible, bone-shaking experience: The most pathetic looking man in the world gives me a smile of recognition. The Most Pathetic Man In The World has huge horn-rimmed spectacles and buckteeth; he's wearing a dirty fawn anorak and brown cord trousers which have been rubbed smooth at the knee; he, too, is being taken to see Howard's End by his parents, despite the fact that he's in his late twenties. And he gives me this terrible little smile because he has spotted a kindred spirit. It disturbs me so much that I can't concentrate on Emma Thompson and Vanessa and the rest, and by the time I rally, it's too late and the story's too far down the road for me to catch up. In the end, a bookcase falls on someone's head.

His description of the other man rather vividly paints a picture of how he sees himself. It also points out how humor is so close to sadness. His desultory description of how the picture ends also illustrates the character's state of mind. The bookcase falling on Fred's head or Mary's head is not funny. Falling on someone's head is, because the character hasn't paid attention and doesn't give a damn.

Before leaving this chapter, we should examine the use of proper names for characters. After we read a book, it most always seems the author chose the right names for the characters. But if you're anything like I am and like most authors I know are, choosing a name for a character is a chore. I scour the phone book for days, and even after selecting a name I tend to change it unless it feels absolutely right. Evelyn Waugh, in *Decline and Fall*, uses the following names, and I daresay there isn't one of them that isn't highly satirical: *Mr. Sniggs, Mr. Postlewaite, Sir Alastair Digby-Vaine-Trumpington, Lord Pastmaster, Margot Beste-Chetwynde,*

Cluttebuck, Dr. Fagan, Mr. Paul Pennyfeather, The Earl of Circumference, Colonel Side Boham, and last, *Otto Friedrich Selenus.* Is there any doubt about the seriousness of this book?

I think it is very important to name your characters so that the reader finds the names natural and quite appropriate. I wish I could tell you how that's done.

Exercise: Write a two-page character outline of a regular person. Then try to put that person into a situation where things go terribly wrong so the reader, not the character, thinks it funny.

Exercise: Take the same character and this time make him/her humorous. In other words create someone about whom, if we met in real life, we would say: "What a character."

Exercise: Make a list of character traits that best describe a humorous character.

4

The Incidental Character

I can't remember your name, but don't tell me.
—ALEXANDER WOOLLCOTT

MANY WRITERS RESIST USING ANY HUMOR AT ALL simply because they are afraid that their serious theme will be adulterated by it. I think their concern is justified. You can't force humor onto characters who are involved with serious issues, especially if those characters are not prone to making light of anything.

The problem with this kind of book is this: It can become unreadable. Page after page of unremitting seriousness demands two elements: 1. A damn fine writer. 2. A damn fine reader – one who's willing to reread paragraphs again and again.

Serious writers may realize their work is dense and hard to read, but they don't know what to do to lighten the load. And, as I said before, they're fearful of changing their characters' attitudes as it may adulterate the serious tone.

Their fear is unjustified. However, by using a simple technique they can relieve the unremitting heavy tone if they wish, e.g.: The main character or characters encounter someone who, oblivious to their travails, makes light conversation or is involved in a humorous situation. The contrast is even more evident when your serious character doesn't respond and, in fact, treats the incident with indifference.

The Incidental Character Example:
The young couple in a restaurant discuss their impending divorce when the waiter interrupts to tell them the ridiculously named specials for the night. The waiter leaves and the couple resume their conversation. A second later the waiter returns and informs them the kitchen is out of all the specials except one. This time they order from the menu and sigh with relief when the waiter leaves again. They continue on until the dinner comes. She is near tears. He is angry. The dinner arrives and they discover the waiter has the order wrong. They accept the dinners so they can get on with their discussion. A moment later they both laugh at the inefficient waiter. The serious mood has been broken, but soon after the laugh, they resume their discussion.

Now this may be too much. But you can see how the waiter character and the ensuing action is a counterpoint to their very painful conversation. The writer who wishes to maintain a credible tone for the main characters, yet senses that some degree of relief is needed, must look to the incidental character. Of course it is imperative to introduce that character in the most natural way. And you must take care that the character's action and dialogue fit appropriately into the fabric of the work. (It won't do to have some yahoo come into the book, tell a bad joke, and leave.)

It also helps if your incidental character has some character traits that distinguish him. That is, make the person more than a generic waiter, policeman, etc. Take care to give the reader a visual picture. Think of a scene in a movie where the romantic leads encounter an ice cream vendor in the park. Now think of the vendor as John Cleese. When you translate this picture into language, you now have a character who has an attitude. It doesn't matter that he only says, "Vanilla or chocolate – that'll be two dollars." Your remarks about him, or the main characters' reactions, will give added life to an otherwise ordinary scene.

Look at old movies on TV, especially light comedies or musicals. You'll see a host of incidental characters who became famous as supporting players. They were called character actors for one good reason. There was no need for any exposition, as the audience knew them for what they were. And they seldom changed, no matter what movie they were in. Franklin Pangborn was the fussy, flustered hotel manager or the blinking civil servant. Eugene Paulette, the brisk business man or the huffy father. Elijah Cook, Jr., the baby-face killer or the stool pigeon. Try to think of these actors as prototypes when you need a humorous incidental character. Remember, there are no small parts, just small actors. Try to make their brief appearance in your story as interesting as you can. Don't let your recently divorced person who just faced the IRS under suspicion of tax fraud get in a cab and have the driver just say, "Where to?"

More difficult then the incidental character is the incidental event. This is where your serious character or characters become involved with something that is humorous to the reader but not necessarily to the characters. In this scenario great care must be taken so that the event doesn't appear hokey or artificial. It is usually something that happens to them that is beyond their control, e.g.: The 4:30 train, which is usually a local, has been suddenly changed to an express and the characters whiz by their stop at fifty miles an hour, thus making them late for a date with their psychologist; e.g.: The romantic winter cabin, miles from nowhere, has a clogged chimney in the fireplace as its only source of heat.

The main idea is to have an external happenstance inflict itself on your characters. If there were one word to describe either of these conditions it would be "conflict." Someone or something goes wrong, and the resolution of the problem creates the humorous situation. The process of resolving the conflict results in a scene, an episode. And it is revealed to the reader either by dialogue or narrative.

There is one other genre in the incidental category. That is when the work itself presents a humorous environment where the characters are serious. Any farce by Moliere presents this scenario. The machinations of the plot make it impossible for the characters not to appear humorous. They are trapped by the author's diabolical scenario, and it is their effort to escape their fate that creates the conflict.

Exercise: Create a scene where two characters begin a serious conversation and a third character, oblivious to their situation, intervenes in a humorous way.

Exercise: Create a scene where your character or characters are faced with an external event that has humorous connotations, e.g.: the train situation; the stuck-somewhere situation.

Exercise: Create a scene where one character with serious intent is thwarted by an incidental humorous character.

5

Dialogue

It's our fault. We should have given him better parts.

—JACK WARNER

(on hearing that Ronald Reagan had been elected governor of California)

OSCAR WILDE COMES TO MIND when I think of dialogue. The epigrams, the ripostes and wit. Does your dialogue have to measure up to those brilliant standards? You'll be relieved to know that unless you're writing a drawing room comedy, the answer is no. But you do have to be sure that your characters don't indulge in everyday conversation throughout the piece. When asked why he thought his books moved along so well, Elmore Leonard said that he left out the parts the readers skip. It's important to remember that dialogue is what your characters say and not what you say. There are subtle and not so subtle differences in how people think and talk, and the writer, once the character is established, must keep them consistent throughout the work.

I believe a lot of writers think that reality is simulated by having their characters go through the routines of life in a complete fashion. When I worked as a story editor for Jack Webb of "Dragnet" fame, his idea of verisimilitude was to have the characters talk about very ordinary things. Take ordering a hamburger and then comparing, ad infinitum, the merits of those particular burgers to several others throughout the city:

FRIDAY: I don't think these buns are as good as Harry's down on Third.

COP: It's not the bun, it's the relish. There's no zest to the relish.

FRIDAY: That burger we had in Santa Monica last week was pretty damn good.

COP: Except for the pickle. I found the pickle wanting.

This would go on for two more pages. Does this make their characters more believable? I think not. Could two people have this conversation? I'm afraid so. Does it belong in a book or short story? I hope not. John Fowles wrote: "If you want to be true to life, start lying about it." Here is a major pronouncement: Dialogue is the author's version of what's going on rather than a realistic portrait. And good dialogue, humorous dialogue, is credible and therefore doesn't suspend disbelief. It is important for the writer in the context of the story to have the reader believe the characters would say what they're saying.

Most humorous dialogue relies on three key elements: surprise, exaggeration, and sarcasm. The surprise element, most of the time, is constructed like a good joke. The setup, the embellishment or development, and the punch line. The character then says something you don't expect. When it comes to dialogue, Elmore Leonard is a master. He applies the same principle to his dialogue as he does to the narrative. He leaves out the parts that people skip. His characters do not have everyday conversations that faithfully report minute-to-minute events. So when Mr. Leonard eliminates the superfluous gab he accentuates the reality and creates drama. Here's an excerpt from *Get Shorty*. Chili Palmer, a likable hood, is talking to a has-been movie producer:

"It's like saying you know where a movie star lives, being on the in."

Harry said, "I know where all kinds of movie stars live. It doesn't do a thing for me."

Chili said, "Yeah? I wouldn't mind driving past some of their homes sometime."

"You know who used to live right here? Cary Grant."

"No shit. In this house?"

"Or was it Cole Porter. I forget which."

The inside joke is that the producer has mixed up Cary

Grant with Cole Porter because Mr. Grant played Cole Porter in a movie supposedly about Mr. Porter's life. It isn't supposed to be a laugh riot, but it certainly tells us something about Harry, the producer. Here's an example from Carl Hiaasen's *Stormy Weather*:

> *"Are those your puppies?... They sound adorable – what kind?"*
> *"Fertilizer hounds," he said.*
> *"Fertilizer hounds?"*
> *"When I get done with 'em, yeah."*

The Confederacy Of Dunces, by John Kennedy Toole, is full of delightful surprises in the dialogue. Here is one example:

"I dust a bit," Ignatius told the policeman. "In addition I am at the moment writing a lengthy indictment against our century. When my brain begins to reel from my literary labors, I make an occasional cheese dip."

I don't know about you, but I sure didn't expect the cheese dip line, and the absurdity of it made me smile. Again it's the setup, the development – in this case it is more effective by word usage: the brain reeling from literary labors – that sets up the quite unsuspected punch line. It wouldn't be funny if he had said, "I take a walk in the park." Why? Because it is a normal thing to do. I think it important to add that Ignatius didn't say the cheese dip line to be funny. He was quite sincere, which made it all the funnier and made him a humorous character. Here is a piece of dialogue

Writing Humor

from *Decline And Fall*, by Evelyn Waugh. Without a doubt, if one may use the word droll, this example is droll. It is also very British:

He is not the son-in-law I should readily have chosen. I could have forgiven him his wooden leg, his slavish poverty, his moral turpitude, and his abominable features; I could even have forgiven him his incredible vocabulary, if only he had been a gentleman. I hope you do not think me a snob. You may have discerned in me a certain prejudice against the lower orders. It is quite true. I do feel deeply on the subject. You see, I married one.

Dialogue can also be non sequitur. That is, it can avoid rational meaning altogether. There are so many American humor writers who excel at this sort of thing. My favorites are Robert Benchley, S.J. Perelman, and James Thurber.

Here is an example from Woody Allen. The short story is called "The Whore Of Mensa." We're in the office of a private eye named Kaiser Lupowitz, and the new client is explaining his problem:

"I'm a working guy," he said. "Mechanical maintenance. I build and service joy buzzers. You know – those little fun gimmicks that give people a shock when they shake hands?"
"So?"
"A lot of your executives like 'em. Particularly down on Wall Street."

The setup is mechanical maintenance. You think elevators,

washing machines, etc. You certainly don't expect joy buzzers, and that's the key to that joke. This is a good example of two elements of humorous dialogue: surprise and exaggeration. The surprise element, most of the time, is constructed like a good joke, which is the setup, the embellishment or development, and the punch line. The character then says something you don't expect. Woody Allen, in the short story "The Macabre Accident," writes a classic example of this technique:

The Setup:

"I just shot my husband," wept Cynthia Freem as she stood over the body of the burly man in the snow."

The Development:

"How did it happen?" asked Inspector Ford getting right to the point.

"We were hunting. Quincy loved to hunt, as did I. We got separated momentarily. The bushes were overgrown. I guess I thought he was a woodchuck. I blasted away. It was too late."

The Punch Line:

"As I was removing his pelt, I realized we were married."

The next few lines are not so structured. They defy logic and are purposely bizarre. It has a surrealistic quality and a Marx Brothers' style. S.J. Perelman and Woody Allen are masters of this kind of writing. And it can be very funny, but the writer must be careful not to go too far. Then it can become tedious and artificial. In short, you just can't join a bunch of non sequiturs together as a successful technique.

Inspector Ford examined the dead man's possessions. In his pocket there was some string, an apple from 1904 and instructions on what to do if you wake up next to an Armenian.

"Mrs. Freem, was this your husband's first hunting accident?"

"His first fatal one. Yes. Although once in the Canadian Rockies, an eagle carried off his birth certificate."

"Did your husband wear a toupee?"

"Not really. He would carry it with him and produce it if challenged in an argument...."

You can see how effective this is, especially after the more logical setup. Mr. Allen did throw in one joke: When asked if it were her husband's first accident, she replies his first fatal one. But I hope you can also understand that ten pages of this could stop being humorous. The toupee line and birth certificate line are, as they say, left fielders. Left fielders can work some of the time, but you must be careful not to overuse them. My theory for this is that most of the time humor must have some base to rest on, some prejudicial knowledge that the reader can recognize and relate to.

The next example of good dialogue also paints a vivid picture of a social group. It's from a short story by James Thurber called "Tea at Mrs. Armsby's." Mr. and Mrs. Monroe have arrived at an afternoon tea after going to a cocktail party where Mrs. Monroe had one too many:

"My husband," said little Mrs. Monroe, "is a collector."

This statement surprised no one more than Mr. Monroe, who was not a collector.

"And what do you collect, Mr. Monroe?" asked Mrs. Armsby, politely.

"Handkerchiefs," said Mrs. Monroe. "He collects handkerchiefs."

It was apparent to Mr. Monroe that his wife's remarkable statements were the unfortunate result of their attending a cocktail party before dropping in, late, at Mrs. Armsby's. The teas which Mrs. Armsby gave on Sundays were the sort at which tea was served...

[Then after a bit:]

"My husband also collects pencils," said Mrs. Monroe. It was warm in the room. The closeness of the air had, as it were, 'got to' Mrs. Monroe. One saw this....

"My husband has eight hundred and seventy-four thousand pencils," said Mrs. Monroe.

"Really?" said Mrs. Penwarden, with evident interest.

"I became interested in pencils in the Sudan," said Mr. Monroe. "The heat is so intense there that it melts the lead in the average Venus or Faber–"

"Or Flaber," said his wife.

"Or Flaber, as the natives call it," continued Mr. Monroe. "The native Sudanese pencil, or vledt, will resist even the most terrifying hea – even oxyacetylene. My vledt formed the basis for my collection, which is now of a certain minor importance, perhaps...."

[In a moment where the attention shifts to someone else.]

"I want to lie down," said Mrs. Monroe.

"I'll get your things," said her husband. "Try not to lie down till I get your things."

Hurriedly, Mr. Monroe left the room and brought back his wife's coat and handbag.

"My things," said Mrs. Monroe, with bewildering dignity.

A perfect picture of the scene, of Mr. and Mrs. Monroe, and as I wrote before, a very astute observation of human behavior. While it is very funny, one can see that Mr. Monroe loves his wife very much as he decides to go along with her. You can also see that Mr. Thurber writes very simply, nothing fancy. Would the piece be as funny if Mr. Monroe, instead of playing along, were angry with his wife and refuted everything she said? It depends. Husband-and-wife confrontations can be quite amusing. Even the scathing *Who's Afraid of Virginia Woolf* has a lot of very funny moments. But if Thurber had written it that way, we would miss the touching aspect of their relationship.

If you keep it simple, short, and to the point, you will write good humorous dialogue. After you write it, test it by saying it out loud without tripping over your tongue. The most difficult technique in writing dialogue is to give each character a unique way of saying things without resorting to obvious tricks. I believe the best way to do this is by not trying to do it. Zen? Perhaps. But if you know your characters well, the words they speak will be quite natural. In other words, allow the characters to be themselves.

In *Practical Demon Keeping*, Rachel is visited by Catch, a demon:

"We tried to call you up at the meeting last week, but I didn't think it worked because I didn't draw the circle of power with a virgin blade that had been quenched in blood."

"What did you use?"

"A nail file."

"I'm sorry," she said, "but it's not easy to find a blade that's been quenched in blood."

Catch says: "I will need you to renounce the Creator and perform a ritual. In return you will be given the command of a power that rules the Earth. Will you do this?"

Rachel could not believe what she was hearing. She wasn't sure her career in exercise instruction had prepared her for this.

The subject of this conversation is handled in a most ordinary way. But the author comments in the last line about Rachel's career in exercise instruction. Without this comment, the reader could assume this conversation is quite serious. The excerpt points out that your characters do not think of themselves as funny. It is the attitude of the author that accents the humor.

If the character has a foreign accent, you have two choices. You can phonetically spell out the pronunciation (puleeeze) or you can manipulate the syntax (The train, it is coming here on time?). To my mind, each method is perilous inasmuch as both can become quite tiresome to the reader unless they are judiciously handled. My personal choice would be method number two. Better still, have your foreign-accented characters speak better English. There is one exception to all of the above. If your character needs an accent to complete the portrayal in a comedic way, then go for it. Utilize one or the other method or even both together as in the example below.

PNIN
by Vladimir Nabokov

"Eighteen, 19," muttered Pnin. "There is not great difference! I put the year correctly, that is important! Yes, I still need 18 – and send me a more effishant card when 19 available."

Epigrams, Aphorisms and Ripostes:

You'll be relieved to know these weapons, though very effective and even memorable, are not necessary for your dialogue arsenal. If you look in most dictionaries of humorous quotations, you'll see a great percentage of the entries are from writers long dead. Oscar Wilde leads the pack. "Caricature is the tribute that mediocrity pays to genius," is one of hundreds. Oscar Levant, great wit and pianist, said: "An epigram is only a wisecrack that's played Carnegie Hall."

If you decide your character can utter these kinds of lines, best to be quite sure they hit the mark and the character deserves them. This isn't to say that only highly sophisticated characters are allowed this kind of remark. Will Rogers, the bucolic humorist and performer, was famous for his pithy and devastating lines about the human condition. Here is one, appropriate for this chapter: "In Hollywood the woods are full of people that learned to write but evidently can't read; if they could read their stuff, they'd stop writing."

One last word on dialogue. Characters, no matter their station in life, no matter their IQs, their education, inevitably respond to all situations from the heart. When the genius physicist accidentally pounds a hammer into his thumb he cries, "Oh shit."

Narrative

The covers of this book are too far apart. —AMBROSE BIERCE

THE NICE THING ABOUT THE NARRATIVE VOICE is the author can watch the characters and make comment. You can approve, disapprove, chide, chastise, and gloat. They can be in the most difficult situations, but that third person sits comfortably somewhere above and only intervenes when the author chooses. And instead of the characters talking, it is you.

The opportunity for humor in the narrative is infinite. In depends on the choice of words, the style, of the author. The following is a rewritten paragraph stolen from S.J. Perelman. It offers the same information as the original. See if you can tell the difference:

For the casual visitor in London, one who enjoys a hotel that isn't fancy and is reasonable in price, few hotels can beat Peacock's, in Clarges Street. Besides the reasonable rates, they offer good service and good plain food.

Now here is the S.J. Perelman version:

For the casual visitor in London averse to ostentation and uncushioned by expense account, few hotels offer the advantages of Peacock's, in Clarges Street. Its rates are modest and its service amiable, its cuisine, by and large, free of the viscous sauces that agglutinate the English menu.

The precise choice of words tells the story. The writer and TV producer Norman Lear once said: "All humor, basically, is based on conflict." As you can see, the first version is straight reporting with little personality. Mr. Perelman's version makes comment. Same idea, big difference.

I'd say that one needs to perfect the narrative voice. A funny world is easier to deal with than funny characters. Lyrical and funny narrative writing is damn hard to do and very time consuming compared to writing dialogue. I also think that writing humor or comedy is something that one must do all the time, not just when one is sitting in front of the machine. A take-along notebook is an important thing for the comedy writer. I've carried funny lines for up to ten years waiting for the right fictional circumstances to plug them in. –CHRISTOPHER MOORE

Another example of how narrative sets the tone is in Laurence Shames's fine mystery novel *Florida Straits*. This descriptive paragraph is mean and yet it is very funny:

The first thing that Joey noticed about his half brother Gino Delgatto – noticed from thirty feet away – was that his new girlfriend had enormous breasts. They started about three inches below her shoulders, then billowed out and down, but mostly out, tapering only slightly as they went, with the jolly, bouncy, cozy taper of small blimps. You could have run raft trips down her cleavage. Measured against these monumental bosoms, the girlfriend's features could only appear ungenerous and pinched, the eyes smallish in spite of all the tricks to make them bigger, the narrow nose barely equal to the job of sucking in air, the mouth, for all its caked on lipstick, as austere as a mail slot. Gino did not think to introduce her. He would as soon have introduced a new settee.

Mr. Shames begins by telling us the first thing Joey noticed about his half brother was this woman. (A nice off-kilter joke.) From that point on Joey has nothing to do with what follows. If you read the whole novel you'll find that Joey hasn't the capacity to compare her lips to an austere mail slot. It is the author who takes over, and we are grateful for his comic voice. Mr. Shames's narrative tone matches his New York wise-guy characters perfectly.

So many times your characters are not as clever as you are. (Most writers will agree with that.) The trick is to insert your observations, your wit and sensibilities into the narrative as unobtrusively as possible. It is also important for the writer to make narrative and dialogue of a similar tone. If your characters are simple country folk and your narrative is pure Noel Coward you have a problem. Read any of Ian Fleming's James Bond novels and you'll see how Mr. Bond and Mr. Fleming easily blend. But let us say you have a character unlike anyone else in the book. Do you change the narrative voice to suit that character? I think not. Let the character's dialogue illuminate the difference. And whenever possible, if the character has a dialect, try not to spell the words as they might sound. Yes, I know. A lot of very good writers use odd spelling to illustrate dialect. 'Nuff said.

A recent *New Yorker* review by Mary Hawthorne of a book called *Le Mariage,* by Diane Johnson, brought up this interesting point:

She is far more interested in how particular character types interact with one another in what often prove to be absurd situations than she is in deep psychological analysis.... In the end, it's Johnson's insights that account for the charm of these books, not her characters.

I think this is the first time I have ever read where the author's intrusions seem more important than the characters. Most readers, when talking about a book, talk about the characters and the story. And when they talk about the author, it is in the sense of their ability to create the work.

Using analogies in the narrative is another great tool for the writer. The only trouble with them is they're hard to write and when they're bad, they really are bad. Nick Hornsby in

High Fidelity has a beauty:

I had to nurture those doubts as if they were tiny, sickly kittens, until eventually they became sturdy, healthy grievances, with their own cat doors, which allowed them to wander in and out of our conversation at will.

One wonders if there ever has been a successful book that excludes the author's opinions. Perhaps Ernest Hemingway's books with their matter-of-fact narrative style come close. But Mr. Hemingway's pervasive style might, in itself, be evidence of the author's strong personality. I don't think any other writer has more contests where the contestants emulate his writing style. Most of the time we expect the third-person narrative voice to have a personality but not to the extent it overshadows the characters. It certainly is a necessity when it comes to writing humor.

This is especially true when the characters (see chapter 4) have no idea they're funny. The writer should not rely on the intrinsic humor of the situation to get the point across. She must let us know that she's aware of the humor and let us know by her sly wink as she describes the scene. In Mary Hawthorne's review she also writes: "We sense an impish wink to the reader." This emphasizes the importance for the writer to set a tone or style that is unmistakably humorous. If the reader doesn't get the hint, there's a good chance the writing will fail.

I suppose you might say there's a style to all narrative writing. Each of us has developed speech patterns over the years, and I'm sure these patterns occur when you write. But to try for a writing style is a dangerous ambition. When the reader becomes more aware of style than content, the writer has gone too far. By virtue of who we are, who we were, and our likes and dislikes, we all have a style whether we're conscious of it or not. There are certain writers who have a distinctive way of writing who may be called stylists. Thomas Wolfe comes to mind. William Faulkner to a slightly lesser degree. But neither one, to my mind, writes in a style that negatively affects the work. Style is like background music in a movie: If you notice it too much, it isn't good.

The writer should have a personality but not to the extent that the reader feels he's shouting, "Look at me! Look at me!" The question is how to obtain this narrative ease. I call it ease because there are writers who seem to make their narrative flow in such a natural way, you're turning pages one after the other without realizing it. I don't wish to imply you should *dumb down* the writing to make it easy to read. On the other hand, try to read some academic journals where the authors purposefully create long complex sentences with obscure language to show off their incredible intelligence and hopefully befuddle the reader enough to fool them into thinking they're just not getting it when, in fact, there's nothing there to get. OK, the last sentence made sense, but here's one with which I can't compete. This is an example from the second-prize winner of the *Philosophy and Literature Journal's* inadvertent bad writing contest. I chose this one as it was written by a professor of English. His name will mercifully be withheld. I quote verbatim:

If, for a while, the ruse of desire is calculable for the uses of discipline soon the repetition of guilt, justification, pseudo-scientific theories, superstition, spurious authorities, and classifications can be seen as the desperate effort to "normalize" formally the disturbance of a discourse of splitting that violates the rational, enlightened claims of its enunciatory modality.

This would be humorous if it weren't so tragically real. If professors of English write this way, their students are in real trouble.

Style has nothing to do with showing off. The narrative should be clear, precise, and honest, without pretension or conceit. The writer should be careful not to start too many sentences with the same words. The writer should look at the length of sentences and vary the rhythm of words. The writer, etc....There is a rhythm to good writing, and I suggest the way to find it is by reading to yourself out loud. You may also record the words or have someone read them to you.

This excerpt is from *Fried Green Tomatoes at the Whistle Stop Café,* by Fannie Flagg:

About ten years ago, when Ed had started seeing a woman he worked with down at the insurance company, she had attended a group called The Complete Woman, to try and save her marriage. She wasn't sure she loved Ed all that much, but she loved him just enough to not want to lose him. Besides, what would she do? She had lived with him as long as she had lived with her parents. The organization believed that women could find complete happiness if they, in turn, would dedicate their entire lives to just making their men happy.

Of course, even though she was not religious, it was a comfort to know that the Bible backed her up in being a doormat.

So, hoping she was on the right track, she started up the ladder on the Ten Steps To Complete Happiness. She tried step number one and met Ed at the front door nude, wrapped in Saran wrap. But Ed had been horrified. So she never tried step number two; going to his office dressed as a prostitute. Later on, still looking, she tried to get involved with the Women's Community Center. She liked what they stood for, but secretly wished they would wear just a little lipstick and shave their legs.... She had wanted to belong, but when the woman suggested that next week they bring a mirror so they could study their vaginas, she never went back.

The above paragraph uses a reliable comedic technique. Ms. Flagg is comparing innocence with something naughty. It is usually inspired by someone's desire to do something daring to please another. Born of desperation, the character is ready to stray from the usual path and try something different. This creates the conflict, which, in turn, creates the humor. In this case, there is also an inner conflict. There is a limit to the character's acquiescence, and so we have the line: "...she never went back."

In writing good narrative you should also be particularly aware of the type of subject you are describing. Different places, scenes, situations, always clue the writer to what is appropriate. Perhaps the descriptive phrases about a beautiful panorama should be long and flowing, while dramatic action can be written in short, thrifty sentences. The humorous narrative shouldn't have complex phrases full of asides, hyphens, and dashes. If the reader has to stop to figure things out, you can be sure the light touch will soon turn to lead. Because style is the product of taste and everyone's taste differs, it is near impossible to define. It is not a one-plus-one-equals-two situation. Some authors are so subtle it is a matter of opinion. E.g., I think Elmore Leonard has a unique voice, but it certainly doesn't stand out like Ernest Hemingway's. But my conjecture is that Hemingway did not consciously effect that style. I don't think his rewrites were to try to make it more "Hemingwayish." He was just being himself, and the work evolved from that.

The humorous narrative should also contain an element of surprise. It can be an off-kilter description or a shaggy-dog sentence (a sentence that gives you one or two normal actions, then slips in a strange one). Carl Hiaasen, in *Stormy Weather*, is a master of these techniques:

She spent her days sleeping, **shoplifting** *cocktail dresses and painting her nails.... Edie Marsh headed to Dade County from Palm Beach, where she'd spent six months trying to sleep with a Kennedy...Edie was sure she could do some damage there.* **"Suck 'em cross eyed, then phone the law."**

Then later in the book:

The Naugahyde hissed *as Tony Torres hoisted himself up from the BarcaLounger.*

Through the comic tone of the narrative, Mr. Hiaasen tells us a lot about the characters. Without making judgment, we know the kind of people who own Naugahyde BarcaLoungers. We also know the kind of woman who sleeps all day and steals cocktail dresses. Well, maybe.

Garrison Keillor, in *Lake Wobegon Days*, effects an easy and folksy narrative style that counterpoints the incredible tales he relates as true stories. Mr. Keillor, I'm sure, based his characters on real people, but his deft exaggerations make them both funny and sympathetic:

Suffering was its own reward, to be preferred to pleasure. As Lutherans, we viewed pleasure with suspicion. Birth control was never an issue with us. Nor was renunciation of pleasures of the flesh. We never enjoyed them in the first place.

This is pretty straight reporting until the last line. The technique is perfect. **The Setup**: Suffering was its own reward. **The Development:** The Lutherans, the birth control line, and the renunciation of pleasures of the flesh. **The Punch Line:** We never enjoyed them in the first place. Mr. Keillor follows the same pattern with this line: "Our family was dirt poor, which I figured out as a child from the fact we had such a bad vacuum." **Setup:** Dirt poor. **Development:** Figured out as a child. **Punch:** A bad vacuum. Our family was dirt poor because we had such a bad vacuum doesn't work as well. The formula needs the three ingredients.

Earlier in the book he develops a scene that follows the same pattern. Florian pulls his '66 Chevy into a parking space:

To look at his car, you'd think it was 1966 now, not 1985; it's so new, especially the back seat, which looks as if nobody ever sat there unless they were gift wrapped.... "Got her in '66. Just 42,000 miles on her." It may seem odd that a man should be so proud of having not gone far, but not so odd in this town.

It is a warm and complete picture. Mr. Keillor knows and loves these people and puts us gently into the action without making fun of them or putting them down. At one point in the book he remarks that everyone in town wants to be like everybody else. You don't want to be odd in Lake Wobegon, yet in Mr. Keillor's hands, it is the eccentricities that the reader finds interesting. These are ordinary people doing ordinary things, except the author, by virtue of his narrative style, makes them extraordinary.

Here are a few short excerpts from the brilliant S.J. Perelman:

GENUFLECTIONS IN THE SUN
Two miles south of Corona Del Mar, I saw looming up ahead the Piggy-Wigly Drive-In they had told me in Balboa to watch for. Narrowly missing a Hupmobile driven by an old harpy in curlers, who interpreted my left-hand signal as an invitation to sleep with her, I swerved off the Coast Highway.... A heavy miasma of frying lard and barbecued ribs drifted across the wheel of asphalt radiating from the structure; somewhere inside, the sepulchral voice of Patti Page sniveled a plaint about a doggie in a window.

The old harpy's interpretation of the left-hand signal as

an invitation to sleep with her reminds the modern reader of Woody Allen. And to use the word miasma to describe frying lard and ribs is genius. Most of us would have said "the odor." Why? Because the smell of lard and ribs really doesn't deserve such a word as miasma. It is simply that fact that gives it the humor. It is Mr. Perelman's careful choice of words that makes him a unique writer. And when you think of it, Patti Page did have a sepulchral voice.

In the movie *Born Yesterday,* Judy Holiday's character, Billie, is an uneducated blonde. Her gangster boyfriend hires an English professor to teach her how to talk in a high-class manner so she can pass as a lady. As the movie progresses she tries to use bigger words, but they never seem appropriate to the situation. The results are very funny. It is an ancient comic device. The character is trying to be something she's not. See the second version of the movie, *The Prisoner Of Zenda,* with Peter Sellars. John Cleese, whose interview is later in the book, used the device in *A Fish Called Wanda.*

Look at the following excerpt and pick out the words that give it a humorous tone:

PANTS RECAPTURED
by S.J. Perelman

It was a quarter past one, and Nadine Sanger, torpid from her drugstore lunch of peanut butter on English muffin, sat at the desk in Ezra Vedder's anteroom, listlessly staring at a four-act tragedy in blank verse based on the decline and fall of Montezuma.

There is no doubt in the reader's mind that this is to be

a very satirically funny piece. The writing is urbane and sophisticated and Mr. Perelman's ability to show, don't tell, is exquisite. I would hope you picked *torpid* as one of the clue words. The two names, Nadine Sanger and Ezra Vedder, are carefully chosen. The four-act tragedy would be enough, but Mr. Perelman adds blank verse to sweeten it, then, as a cherry on top, makes the subject Montezuma. Who would read such a play? Indeed, who would write it?

Besides having a delicious sense of humor, S.J. Perelman uses the language in a way that distinguishes him and makes his writing very unique. At the same time, the style doesn't seem forced. I don't think he wrote with a dictionary beside him, and for some reason, although I have no evidence of it, I believe he talked as he wrote, erudite and sophisticated.

The following piece was written for the *Los Angeles Times* by Barry Friedman. It makes a brilliant comment on the writing in art and architecture magazines, but it is also very funny even if the reader has never read that kind of article. This is a great example of satire and a parody of style:

FRANK LLOYD WRIGHT MEETS OSCAR MADISON
ARCHITECTURAL BACHELOR DIGEST: I really can't recall when I've viewed such a shimmering kaleidoscope of tactile interplay and juxtaposition in a single 10-by-12-foot bedroom. It literally shouts "Life!" to me. Really, the sinuous drama of the massive grape juice stain, there contrasted against the stark simplicity of the smashed housefly carcasses lying poignantly on the filthy windowsill here…it's too brilliant. I get a profound sense of functional whimsicality here.

BARRY FRIEDMAN: *The challenge for me was to preserve the integrity of the visual palette without sacrificing surprise and excitement. I wanted to emphasize the flowing quality of space and yet not detract from its innate sense of slovenliness.*

ABD: I particularly love the way you've playfully strewn underwear about.

BF: I'm delighted you noticed. I honestly don't think I could be happy living anywhere where I couldn't have briefs scattered around me. First, there's the sly removal, followed by the raw physicality of actually hurling them into the air, and finally that frozen moment in time when you tingle with the uncertainty of whether they'll land on the floor or succeed in that once-in-a-lifetime shot directly onto a doorknob or ceiling fan. I can't help but feel it's an elasticized art form for the 90s and beyond.

ABD: You've always been an outspoken opponent of ornate furnishings. I wonder if you could expound on the furniture I see here?

BF: Well, it's no secret that I've experimented with a number of both classical and modern styles over the years, but I've come time and time again to an almost Spartan-like approach to furniture. I have a chair, which is buried somewhere underneath that pile of dirty towels, and I have a mattress. By having the mattress only, I have effectively sidestepped the seriousness of a box spring. I find it so...how should I put it?

ABD: May I? It's a refection of a witty minimalism, a pugnacious discontinuity, if you will, that stresses transition and diminishes totality. It's a synergistic interaction that is, possibly, a conscious separation of geometrical perimeters, but more likely a resonant reverberation of compressed, almost Byzantine, inventiveness.

BF: Yeah.

The humor of this piece is doubled if you have ever read the real thing in art magazines. It is a pompous kind of writing that is all show with no regard for clarity or truth. It is exactly the kind of blow-hard dialogue that we mentioned earlier – the pompous jerk character making clichéd assertions as if they were extremely important. I particularly enjoyed the last paragraph, where the magazine gives the most obtuse analysis of a mattress and Mr. Friedman merely replies, "Yeah." Years ago, when I was teaching at UC Irvine, I received an invitation to attend a conference given by a group of sociologists. The only thing I could figure out from the verbiage was that it *was* an invitation. The theme and subjects of the conference were written in socio-speak, and they were incomprehensible to me.

The following short story by E.B. White is parody. The thing that distinguishes it from satire is that Mr. White emulates the writing style of Ernest Hemingway. In other words, he takes a familiar style and copies it in an exaggerated fashion:

"ACROSS THE STREET AND INTO THE GRILL"
by E.B. White

The girl was near enough now so he could smell her fresh receptiveness, and the lint in her hair. Her skin was light blue, like the sides of horses.

"I love you," he said, "and we are going to lunch together for the first and only time, and I love you very much."

"Hello Mr. Perley," she said, overtaken. "Let's not think of anything."

A pair of fantails flew over the sad old Guaranty Trust Company, their wings set for a landing. A lovely double, thought Perley, as he pulled. "Shall we go to the Biltmore on Vanderbilt Avenue, which is merely a feeder lane for the great streets, or shall we go to Schraffts, where my old friend Botticelli is captain of girls and where they have mayonnaise in fiascos?"

"Let's go to Schraffts," said the girl low. "But first I must phone Mummy." She stepped into a public phone booth and dialed true and well, using her finger. Then she telephoned.

Anyone familiar with Hemingway can see the obvious parody. But Mr. White adds some very funny touches. "She said, overtaken" and "mayonnaise in fiascos" are two of my favorites. They both sound as if they are correct usage, just wrong enough to be funny.

The next example is from a short story called "What Brings You to our Fair Land," by Martin Amis:

In the bathroom at the hotel. It was a shaving mirror on a retractable arm.... He thought there must be a lot of people who imagine they look O.K., who fancy they can pass for normal, until they meet a shaving mirror in an American Hotel.... This was the best mirror and it was the worst mirror. All other mirrors were in public relations. After an audience with such a mirror, only two places to go: the plastic surgery or the church.

Mr. Amis writes: "He thought there must be a lot of people who imagine they look O.K." Then there is the last sentence: "After an audience with such a mirror, only two places to go: the plastic surgery or the church." It is still the character's thought, but there is an intrusion by Mr. Amis.

We allow the narrative to sometimes erase the line between the character's voice and the author's. In this case I believe the wry observation is more Martin Amis. What is more important is the fact that the character doesn't merely look in the mirror, but makes comment. The first observation is that a lot of mirrors, perhaps due to tinting, dull lighting, can flatter. But this mirror doesn't lie. The second observation is about the reflection itself. The thought is the character's, but the joke belongs to the author. (I don't think that's clear, but I know what I mean and I hope you do.)

The lesson is obvious. Always look for your character to make comment, to have an attitude or opinions about everything. Of course you don't have to use them all, but save the better ones. They add complexity to the person and make the character more interesting.

It is a less common device when the story is told in the first person. But in case you're thinking of such a beast, you have the chore of not only making the main character funny, but also her observations. Although it is not a laugh riot, *The Adventures Of Augie March*, by Saul Bellow, comes to mind as a good first-person narrative to read; also *Wonder Boys*, by Michael Chabon.

Mark Leyner is a very unique writer. His language is so bizarre, so full of weird thoughts, that I have to read him in small doses. Here are a couple of examples:

TOOTH PRINTS ON A CORN DOG
I'd gone to L.A. to negotiate the purchase of a chain of hernia clinics.... One day, after a particularly grueling morning session

with the seller and our respective attorneys and accountants at
my hotel, the Peninsula in Beverly Hills, needing a respite from
the frustrations of trying to analyze the profit margin on inguinal
rupture repair in light of fluctuating reimbursement caps, and
facing the prospect of an afternoon of poring over truss swatch-
es, I took a stroll around the block.

MY COUSIN MY GASTROENTEROLOGIST

I was driving to Las Vegas to tell my sister that I'd had Mother's
respirator unplugged. Four bald men in the convertible in front
of me were picking the scabs off their sunburnt heads and flick-
ing them on the road... Suddenly as I reached the crest of a hill,
emerging from the fog, there was a bright neon sign flashing on
and off that read: FOIE GRAS AND HARICOTS VERTS NEXT
EXIT.

The field is strewn with the recumbent, softly heaving bodies
of the Chronic Fatigue Syndrome Research Institute's women's
lacrosse team.

And in Lake Tahoe, Angie Dickinson moistens a napkin with
her own spit and wipes hardened tiramisu from the lips of a
quadriplegic chimpanzee she's rescued from an NIH laboratory.

Mr. Leyner has a very strange mind, but he can also teach
us something. While it's wise to carefully choose your words,
sometimes being too careful can paralyze the creative
process. What is commonly called "writer's block" is to my
mind more a case of a writer over editorializing himself.
When everything you write seems unworthy of your
immense talent, it's time to loosen up and get silly. Leynerize

yourself for a few pages. Write it down, show it to a friend. Throw it away.

Earlier I commented on a punch line that Christopher Moore wrote. The analogy was: Homosexuality on Billy was like acne on a leper. Analogies are valuable tools for the humor writer, and I suggest you jot them down whenever you think of them. You never know when they'll come in handy.

Michael Chabon comments on a transvestite's transformation from a woman into a man:

She had assembled her male self with the precision and speed of an assassin in the movies snapping together the parts of his rifle.

The elevator landed like the blow of a hammer in the ground floor of the house.

Her eyes though expressive were badly crossed, and her teeth wandered across her smile like the kernels at the tip of an ear of corn.

And lastly, a metaphor:

I remember that I had been dangling unhappily from the rope of my new life as an English professor....

Exercise: Write ten opening sentences in this style, letting all inhibitions go. Make each sentence as wild and bizarre as you can. Even though they may be of no use, the freedom in writing them may serve you well when you need to find a way to *loosen up* in your work. Remember, if the sentences make perfect sense, you've failed.

Ian Bernard

7

Theme And Subject

MORE AND MORE THESE DAYS it seems that nothing is sacred. But I think the writer should be aware that the darker the subject matter, the thinner the line between acceptance and failure. For our purpose, let's deal with the broader, more generally acceptable spectrum of theme and subject.

Humor can overcome many moods, even tragedy, but the difficulties multiply when you choose themes most people take very seriously. If you can laugh at your own misfortunes, who are we to criticize. But try to write a nonpersonal history of the Holocaust in a humorous way and I'll guarantee you'll fail. You need the autobiographical approach to surmount painful and horrendous subjects.

In my last humor workshop a woman began reading

from a long novel that she explained covered the lives of several Indian tribes. About two pages in we still were waiting for the first humorous line. After another page I stopped her and asked her to tell me the main theme of the book. Her reply was it's about several massacres of Indians throughout America. I asked her why on earth did she want to introduce humor into this very serious book? Her answer was because the book is very depressing.

To paraphrase Mencken: There are no depressing books, only depressing writers. In her case, the problem could not be solved by artificially injecting bits and pieces of humor no matter how artfully done. The main theme of the book had to be modified in order to make such a method possible. To be specific, in this case I recommended she introduce children at play throughout the book. I knew this could have tragic overtones, but at least the reader would have respite from the overall theme.

So what makes a good theme or subject matter for humor? Practically anything that involves the human condition and that includes depravity. (Rabelais and the Marquis De Sade have survived many years.) And I don't think I am contradicting the previous paragraph about the Indian massacres for one important reason. It all depends on how the author handles it.

Where Do Ideas Come From?
The answer is everywhere. Read the newspaper, the magazines, the classifieds. Eavesdrop on conversations in restaurants, bars.

Here are more examples from various publications that I have collected through the years. As bizarre as some of them are, I swear they are all copied as written in the publication. Pick one or two and write a piece stemming from an item:

Note: *The Hollywood Reporter* is a trade paper in Los Angeles that reports the happenings in the movie industry.

Hollywood Reporter: David Carradine starts shooting his "Kung Fuk, The Movie" on Monday.

L.A. Times: YUGOSLAVS PUT EXECUTION OFF. The execution of Andrija Artukovic, a convicted Croatian war criminal, has been postponed indefinitely because of poor health, legal sources said today.

Santa Barbara News Press: MAN DISCOVERED UNDER OUTHOUSE. A Santa Barbara man sitting on crates beneath a woman's outhouse, dressed in plastic, was arrested by rangers.... Rangers hosed off the man and turned him over to the...

L.A. Times: The photo shows a man with sunglasses aiming a rifle. Behind him is another man lining up the shot. The photo caption: *Wearing sunglasses Bob X, a blind hunter, is aided by his brother, Sam, while deer hunting in the woods.*

Vogue: The surprise of Kitty XXX is summed up in her felicitous name. It signals and heralds her correctly. She has a capricious mixture of prettiness and passion, softness and swoop, indifference and a kind of whimsical sensuality, and conveys with every springing movement the message that life, to her, is an enormous exploration, that the world is at her feet and that she may, or may not tread gently. Anxious that she should not be thought of as merely a pretty face, she describes how she uses her mind with a charming disregard for the implicit, while ninety percent of her listeners simply look at her skin, like the inside of a peony petal, or watch her eyes: big, glowing, musky, the whites slightly blue, eyelashes drooping with their own weight.

Hotel menu: In the heart of Kansas, in a dry town of five thousand with thirty churches. Party Calendar for their singles get-together on Friday nights. Item 22 on the activity menu: *Blow Jobs $1.00*...(It was a nonalcoholic drink.)

New York Post: Nab Suspect as Enema Bandit. Police charged Robert XXX with the armed robbery of two coeds who were also administered enemas by the masked assailant.

Ad in *TV Guide*: *Tortured 9 years by 2 Corns and a Wart.*

Poster for a charity dance: *Dance Away Birth Defects.*

A restaurant review from the weekly paper in Laguna Beach: *Located on top of the tallest structure in town, the elegant setting overlooks the city from a vantage point which has surf lapping at its feet. With appointments which are unusual in this day and age, their menu has a varied choice of offerings from the sea or shore. But, after arriving before your reservation time, do have a treat in the small cocktail ante-room which is cozy as at home in front of your own fireplace. Or join in the conversation at the bar where hometown news and international politics are spoken with equal familiarity. Rack of Lamb done to your choice (ours is well done) tops the listing of favorites. We are not able to finish the meal under most conditions, it is so rich and elegant.*

Ad in *New York Post: KUNDALINI AWAKENING IN 10 DAYS. If Kundalini is not awakened, complete refund.*

An emergency-exit card on a plane: *Passengers in exit rows should identify themselves to a crew member if they cannot read, speak, or understand English.*

New York Times: …reported a case of a man who injected cocaine into his penis to heighten sexual pleasure.… The last time he did so he suffered a persistent painful erection that lasted three days, prompting him to seek medical help.… During a bath, his gangrenous penis fell off.

Headline in Newport Beach paper in California: *WORK ON GROINS STARTS MONDAY.*

Headline from same paper: *DR. SLY WILL BE SPEAKER IN ORANGE.*

Question in "Ask the Doctor" column: *H.M. writes: Could dying hair cause insanity in a 43-year-old woman?*

The Hollywood Reporter: "The Great Life" by George Christy…

They live comfortable among all the silver and gold and paintings. What's nice is they use the silver and gold...one of the gold tureens which belonged to Napoleon is used for serving soup. Don't you hate it when people lock up everything that's precious and lose touch with reality.

New York Post headline: SCHHMUCK AND BIGHAM VOWS WILL BE READ.

Hollywood Reporter: She also said he constantly criticized her face and body, humiliated her in public and, during sex, appeared to fantasize about other women.

Sports-page item: Dick Trickle won his first Winston Cup pole position.

News item: Kirstin Harquist wore a name tag that read "Sally Brown" as she greeted customers at Nordstroms. Harquist explained that all hostesses wear the name "Sally Brown."

News item: INTIMATE APPAREL SHOW DRAWS 700 TO OPENING.

More news items:

Part time girl to work mornings.

Costuming – a feature for which the ballet company has already become noted – will again be in evidence.

GRADUALISM NOW!

Fossilized dinosaur dung contains evidence that flatulence from the giant creatures may have helped warm Earth's climate.

And lastly, and item from the Beverly Hills Courier: A man who tried to hold up a bank on Wilshire Boulevard was foiled by a conscientious teller who told him she needed to see his ID before she would hand over the money.... The flabbergasted bandit replied, "Don't you understand, I'm a robber." The teller, a US resident for only two years, said she didn't know what he meant and still asked to see some identification.

Any one of these items is ripe for comment or expansion. Everyday life presents the writer with a myriad of ideas. You just have to be open to them.

I'll list a few subjects that Dave Barry has written on in the past:
- Food for thought – his son enters a science fair at school
- Father faces life – a long-overdue attack on natural childbirth
- Pumped up – too many kinds of sneakers
- Dirty dancing – his son going to dances
- A left-handed compliment – left handers have shorter lives
- Watch your rear – newspaper story about snakes in bathroom
- It's a gas – about Beano

You can readily see that Mr. Barry looks at a variety of topics in a humorous way. If you think there's nothing to write about, you're wrong. There's too much to write about. You just have to read the paper and the magazines.

Exercise: Make a list of things that irritate you in life. (If nothing irritates you, you are either dead or on too much Prozac.) Write a paragraph or two on any or all of the items and exaggerate your points beyond reality. In other words, lie.

Exercise: Take a serious subject and make it humorous. E.g., from Shawn McMurray:

Last December, in order to avoid the hassle and expense of Christmas shopping, I decided instead to opt for double bypass surgery. Contrary to what you might have heard, it's not as much fun as it sounds. . . In my case the path started out with crushing chest pains and arm numbness followed up by frequent nightmares involving all my dead relatives and long tunnels of light. My mother didn't raise any fools, so after only two years of putting up with that inconvenience, I decided to seek medical attention.

Shawn goes on to detail the whole experience. Get the idea?

Exercise: Take any everyday occurrence and give it a twist, an attitude: The PTA meeting, the supermarket, your children, your wife, her relatives.

8

Nonfiction

Of course, "truth is stranger than fiction." Fiction is obliged to stick to possibilities. Truth isn't. —MARK TWAIN

EXCEPT FOR STRAIGHT NEWS REPORTING, I don't believe there is such a thing as true nonfiction. In good nonfiction there are always the enhancing descriptions, the exaggerations, the author's point of view. The four main categories of nonfiction are: 1. The personal-view column (Dave Barry). 2. The sports column. 3. Criticism. 4. And now, thanks to Bill Bryson, travel.

"NOTES FROM A SMALL ISLAND"
by Bill Bryson
If you mention in the pub that you intend to drive from, say, Surrey

to Cornwall, a distance most Americans would happily go to get a taco, your companions will puff their cheeks, look knowingly at each other, blow out air as if to say, "Well, now that's a bit of tall order," and then they'll launch into a lively and protracted discussion of whether it's better to take the A30 to Stockbridge and then the A303 to Ilchester, or the A361 to Glastonbury via Sheptom Mallet. Within minutes the conversation will plunge into a level of detail that leaves you, as a foreigner, swiveling your head in quiet wonderment. "You know that lay-by outside Warminster, the one with the grit box with the broken handle?" one of them will say. "You know, just past the turnoff for Little Puking, but before the B6029 mini-roundabout."

[The discussion goes on and on until they discuss the time of arrival.]

"Well it's entirely up to you of course. But personally if I was planning to be in Cornwall by three o'clock tomorrow, I'd have left yesterday."

Mr. Bryson has written a scene that would be funny on its own, whether or not you have been to England. If you saw this scene in a play or movie, I know you'd laugh. The extra edge is the satirical treatment of the English characters, especially those men who frequent English pubs. I must point out that I strongly suspect this discussion is based on a true happening. What Mr. Bryson did was quite simple. He exaggerated the dialogue just enough to make it very funny. The participants, though, are quite serious. Once the topic is settled – how to get from one place to the other – each man has to outdo the other in his analysis and solution until it reaches a great punch line:

"No, you want to have left a week, last Tuesday."

Is this truly nonfiction? I'm sure the scene happened, but it was Mr. Bryson's treatment that made it so funny. Nonfiction doesn't mean you have to tell the absolute truth.

The following is a dispatch written by Ernest Hemingway in 1922 to the *Toronto Star*:

"A PARIS TO STRASBOURG FLIGHT"
Strasbourg, France September 9, 1922
We were sitting in the cheapest of all the cheap restaurants that cheapen that very cheap and noisy street, the Rue des Petits Champs, in Paris. We were Mrs. Hemingway, William E. Nash, Mr. Nash's little brother and myself. Mr. Nash announced, somewhere between the lobster and the fried sole, that he was going to Munich the next day and was planning to fly from Paris to Strasbourg. Mrs. Hemingway pondered this until the appearance of the Rognons Sautes aux Champignons, when she asked, "Why don't we ever fly anywhere? Why is everybody else always flying and we always stay home?"

That being one of those questions that cannot be answered by words, I went with Mr. Nash to the office of the Franco-Rumanian Aero Company and bought two tickets, half price for journalists, for 120 francs, good for one flight from Paris to Strasbourg. My natural gloom at the prospect of flying, having flown once, was deepened when I learned that we flew over the Vosges mountains and would have to be at the office of the company at five o'clock in the morning. The name Rumanian in the title of the firm was not encouraging, but the clerk assured me there were no Rumanian pilots.

This is a fairly straight piece of reporting but with a couple of pointed remarks that give it a definite attitude: 1. Mrs. Hemingway (not "my wife, Mary") asking why everybody else flies to places and they don't. His use of the formal Mrs. Hemingway indicates a certain forbearance, perhaps a hint of bother. 2. The clerk assuring him there were no Rumanian pilots. 3. The tone of the writing being light, e.g., "Somewhere between the lobster and the fried sole."

What distinguishes this piece from straight reporting is the attitude and the slight exaggerations. Do you really think the airline clerk assured Mr. Hemingway there were no Rumanian pilots? Mr. Hemingway took one of his own legitimate fears and translated it into a very funny line, providing you're not Rumanian.

George Bernard Shaw at one time wrote music criticism and never missed an opportunity to spice the piece up with a few chosen words. A man stopped him on the street during the time he was the music critic for the *London Star*. The man asked him if he knew anything about music. This was Mr. Shaw's answer:

I now take care not to expose my knowledge. When people hand me a sheet of instrumental music and ask my opinion of it, I carefully hold it upside down, and pretend to study it in that position with the eye of an expert. When they invite me to try their

new grand piano, I attempt to open it at the wrong end; and
when the young lady of the house informs me she is practicing the
cello, I innocently ask her whether the mouthpiece did not cut her
lips dreadfully at first....

The column is nothing more than a list of musical mistakes. The lies are so big that if you believe them you are a
fool. What Mr. Shaw is really saying is this: "Are you such
an idiot to think that I'd write music criticism without
knowledge of the subject?" Although at the time the argument was made against Mr. Shaw that a little knowledge
was a dangerous thing, which proves nothing has changed.

Theatrical critics also get a chance to spill some venom.
The famous quip from George Gene Nathan was: "She ran
the gamut of emotions – from A to B."

Here is a sentence from Joan Acocella's review in *The
New Yorker:* "I missed most of the dancing because I could-
n't keep my eyes off Lieberson [an opera singer], who was
declaiming Schubert's 'Erlkonig' as if it were a national
emergency."

Joe Queenan's review of *Hollywood Kids,* by Jackie
Collins, opens this way:

There is a flickering instant in the novel Hollywood Kids *where
Jackie Collins threatens to introduce a principal character that
the average reader might find likable, and even normal. The
character is Michael Scorsinni, a recently wounded New York
cop who has come to Los Angeles to re-establish contact with his
ex-wife, Rita, and 4-year-old daughter, Bella. Scorsinni arrives*

in a city that Ms. Collins has populated with Zane Marion Ricca,
a serial killer; his former employer, Mac Brooks, a movie direc-
tor obsessed with oral sex; Jordanna Levitt, a slut whom Zane is
stalking and whom Brooks seduced when she was 17; Jordan
Levitt, Jordanna's father who drove his first wife and son to suicide;
Kim Levitt, now married to Jordan after a career as a call girl;
Brooks's wife Sharleen, Jordan's ex-lover who is obsessed with oral
sex, preferably in a moving vehicle; and Cheryl Landers, Jordan-
na's best friend, who is pinch-hitting as a brothel operator for a
vacationing friend, who will soon get dressed up as a nurse and
provide Luca Carlotti, Brook's mobster godfather and Zane's uncle,
with the best oral sex he has ever experienced in his whole life.

Mr. Queenan achieves the effect he wants by simply giving us the facts. The effect is rather devastating except to those who are fans of either of the writers. If you read and like Jackie Collins, the review simply lists the kinds of characters you're familiar with. If the paper had given the review assignment to a critic who liked Ms. Collins's work – there just may be such a person – the review may not be humorous. What Mr. Queenan does is to deftly point out that her work is a trifle over the top.

Here's another review from Mr. Queenan:

RAPTOR
by Gary Jennings

Being a hermaphrodite is never easy, even in the best of times,
but it must have been especially difficult in the waning days of
the Roman Empire, when marauding Huns, Vandals, and Goths

were making Europe a hard place for even average people to catch 40 winks and a really tough place for hermaphrodites to relax. The plight of an orphan hermaphrodite is the subject of Gary Jennnings' gargantuan new novel, Raptor, *and a ripping yarn it is.*

There are no jokes. In fact there is no obvious criticism. The subject of the book itself is the grist for the humor. And the line "being a hermaphrodite is never easy even in the best of times" sets the ironic tone. The critic who employs humor usually uses a scalpel rather than a sledge hammer to make the point. It helps if the book has a ridiculous premise or, in the case of Ms. Collins, a cast of unbelievable characters.

The sports column has always been a haven for wise-cracking journalists. The tradition continues. The February 9th, 1999, *Los Angeles Times* had a column by Chris Dufresne, a ski writer, covering the Olympiad in Nagano, Japan, in which he bemoaned the fact that his accommodations were remote and rather high up the mountain:

My pension is located in Tsugaike-Kogen, which I believe in Japanese means nosebleed section.

He further describes the location and the difficulties he encountered. But when it came to reporting on the Olympic events he did so in a matter-of-fact manner. The sports writer has certain restrictions on how far he can go with personal comments when it comes to giving us the facts.

Ian Bernard 123

That doesn't mean the light style disappears completely. There's always the askew adjective to let us know what he thinks. It never is simply, Blue won and White lost and so-and-so scored.

The late Jim Murray, from the *Los Angeles Times*, wrote one of the best and most humorous sport columns. Here are a few short quotes from his column:

Brookline, Mass., for the 1988 U.S. Open golf championship. Welcome to the 1910 open! Please turn your clock back about a century. We're in New England.... I won't say this place is stuffy, but if you ever want to play here, bring your monocle. If your folks came over on the Mayflower, you can get on – for nine holes. The club roster should be a honeycomb. It's full of WASPS. John Kennedy was born here, but if you mention the ex-president, they'll say, "Yes, I knew him and Mrs. Coolidge very well."

St. Louis: It had a bond issue recently and the local papers campaigned for it on the slogan "Progress or Decay." Decay won by a landslide.

Baltimore: The weather is like the team. Gray. Colorless. Drab. The climate would have to improve to be classified as merely lousy. It would be a great place to stage Hamlet, but not baseball games. Baltimore's a great place if you're a crab.

The sports writer has long been famous for sarcasm, quips, and venomous put-downs. Read Ring Lardner or Damon Runyan. They both elevated the sports column to literary heights. There's hardly any humor in merely telling what happened in the game. The good sports writer can accurately report the salient points of the event and leave room for comment about the things that surround it: the crowd, the stadium, the location, the ambiance. The personalities of the participants are also fair game.

The most important elements in sports writing are a distinctive point of view and an attitude. I would suggest as a starter you write about a sport or a sport personality that you don't particularly like.

The personal view column has also spawned quite a few famous names. The advantage to this kind of column is the possibility that the work can be compiled into a book, and so the author gets double service for the same work. Dave Barry and Art Buchwald, two of the best known, are satirists. They pick a topic, usually some timely bit of news, and stray far enough from the reality to make it funny. Aside from their talent as humorists, you can always be sure there is some satirical edge to the writing. In other words, they can be quite serious about the topic and use humor to make the point.

Here are a few sentences from a recent piece by Dave Barry on the Winter Olympics:

I came here to watch the woman's moguls competition, along with 13,500 spectators, several dozen of whom actually saw the event. The rest will not get through security until June at the earliest. The only bad part about the moguls competition was that it was won by a woman from Norway, which, according to the press release I was given, is a foreign country.

Olympic medal update: Hungary is now leading, thanks to a surprise win in the Men's 200 Meter Drive-way Shovel.

We know the security was very tight, but Mr. Barry is suggesting it was so tight as to prevent the customers from actually seeing the event. One can see that the sharp edge to his comments, to some degree, portrayed the reality of the situation.

If you've ever seen Sergio Garcia play golf, you'll notice he stands over the ball and re-grips his club for thirty to forty seconds. One commentator remarked you could read a novel in the time he takes on each shot. The fact that he takes a long time inspired the comment. In any sporting event, someone, either a player or a spectator, offers grist for the humor mill. You just have to look for it.

Personal opinion columns fall into the category of non-fiction, but it's fairly obvious that the amount of exaggeration in most really qualifies them for fiction. The next piece takes a real holiday, a real situation, and jazzes it up beyond the ordinary.

"HAPPY VALENTINE'S DAY: DEAR, HERE'S YOUR MESH BODY STOCKING"
by Ernie Witham

Christmas is officially over. Today I dragged the tree with its fifteen remaining needles out to the curb, tied the Christmas lights into one great big ball like I found them, and dumped the odd remains of two ham-a-ramas and a jalapeño cheese log into the cat's dish, which caused him to immediately jump up onto the telephone stand and look up the address for **the humane society's self-admittance wing.**

[An unabashed joke.]

But it's done. Kaput. Finis. The Yule tide has ebbed. And not a moment too soon, because now it's time for...Valentine's Day. Not to worry though, because this year I'm ready. Last February I was fooled by the pact my wife and I made that we weren't going to bother with Valentine's Day. What I thought she meant was that she didn't expect a gift. What she really meant was that only a chump would think it was okay not to get his wife – who was put on this earth for no greater reason than to serve her husband's every need, although said husband could count on serving certain needs himself until further notice – a gift.

[The above paragraph is the setup for the next sentence, which is the punch line:]

And even though it was quite a bonding experience camping out in my backyard in February with my brother-in-law, who had wondered why everyone was buying flowers on Washington's birthday, I think I'd rather spend the rainy season inside this year.

So I grabbed the garbage bag full of Christmas cards and wrapping paper to drop off at the local landfill, and headed off to the Hallmark store – that magical place full of those beautiful poetic musings that women love. I settled on a card with a romantic, soft-focused photograph of a young couple laughing and hugging in a wooded glen, taken no doubt just seconds before they realized they were standing waist-deep in poison oak. Then I headed across the mall to the lingerie store. The place was

Ian Bernard   127 mobbed with guys all holding intimate apparel, trying to picture their wives in them. One guy was holding his selection upside down, wondering, I suspect, why the thing had snaps at the neck. I was about to explain when a saleslady approached wearing a button that said "All Our Bras Are Half Off." She looked frazzled. Her hair was mussed. Her make-up was smeared, and she had bags under her eyes.

[All bras are half off! Another very good joke.]

"Let me guess," she said. "Gift for the wife?"

Before I could compliment her on such a quick assessment of the situation, she moved me to one side and yelled over my shoulder.

"Please don't mix the satin panties up with the silk ones."

Two guys, who were each holding a dozen pairs of panties, smiled sheepishly, like they just got caught during a midnight raid at the female dorms.

"I hate Valentine's Day," she muttered. Then with a forced smile she asked: "So, what did you have in mind?"

"I dunno. Something sexy, I guess."

"Novel idea. What's her favorite color?"

"Hmm...brown?"

"Brown? Brown's her favorite color?"

"Green?"

"You don't know, do you?"

"Well, our cat is gray and white and she likes him a lot." I thought briefly about the cat and wondered if he'd still be there when I got home. Meanwhile, the saleslady moved me to one side again.

"Sir. Sirrrr."

A large bald man in a three-piece suit glanced up.

"It's Velcro," she said. "As you have no doubt observed, it will make that same sound over and over."

She shook her head, turned her attention back to me, and was about to speak, when a tall, thin guy approached us wearing a teddy over his T-shirt and boxer shorts.

"Whataya think?" he asked.

I thought the red was a little too bright for his complexion and was about to say so when the saleslady jumped up onto a clearance counter and addressed the entire store.

[The innocent question *answered* by the wrong person. This is an ancient comedic device.]

"Okay. Here's what we are going to do. I want every one of you to take out the amount of money you want to spend and step up to the counter. I will hand you an item that costs that amount of money. Do not worry about the color or size. Your wives will be in here to exchange your gifts tomorrow. Now, who's first?"

We all hesitated. She held up her watch.

"The mall closes in fifteen minutes, gentlemen, and they are predicting a particularly cold February this year."

I thought I caught a whiff of damp tent. Then I quickly took out my wallet and got in line.

A reference back to the earlier joke about sleeping outside. Many sitcoms use this trick, setting up a joke in act one and then repeating it in act two.

So here we have a beginning, a middle, and an end. It's like a scene in a movie. In fact, if you ever wish to write this kind of piece, that's the best way to think of it. You set the scene and the situation – one that can have a resolution –

and then put yourself into it. It's wise to have the end in mind before starting, as it is pretty important to have a punch line at the end. Note: Most opinion columns are about the author. Rarely do you find one that paints a portrait of someone else. The other important thing to note is the author is usually self-deprecating. The conflict is the author against the world. It can be nature, society, gadgets, trends, fashion, whatever. If you think everything is just fine, don't write this kind of piece. It won't be funny.

One of my favorite kinds of writing in nonfiction is the first-person telling of problems: the whining, bitching, angry, frustrated man. This short story, very much like the humorous column, springs from a very real situation, but through exaggeration and fantasy becomes something much more than a nonfiction piece.

"BRAIN ON A BIG SCREEN"
by Dean Opperman

Recently, I had fears for my own sanity. I had concluded it was normal to question one's mental health at thirty days sobriety. But now it had been three years since I'd had a drink and still I felt that my brain was like a newborn puppy in need of house-training. While possessed of a certain antic intelligence, it's in need of constant discipline.

My sponsor shook his head. "Damn it, Opperman, how many times do I have to tell you? Your thoughts don't mean a thing! It's your actions that matter. I'll bet there isn't a single person on Earth who would like to have all their thoughts placed on a big screen for everyone to see."

I laughed, but the idea intrigued me. All my thoughts on a big screen? Could I do that? Would I let the general public see everything that crosses my mind during the course of a day? Of course not. It would be totally embarrassing. I doubt that a thousand future space probes will ever scan terrain as bizarre and forbidding as the panorama behind my eyeballs.

[The premise:]

This morning is a case in point. Now, typically, I get out of bed around 7:30 a.m. Unfortunately, my brain gets up about 7. He's already showered, shaved and sitting on the couch waiting for me to wake up. His mission – kill me. Again, I was naked in the arms of the phenomenal dark-haired beauty named Candy.

"Dean, darling, whatever you do, don't stop." She kissed me again and again. "Never stop, Dean. You are fantastic. I love you more than life itself."

I wanted to make love to her again, but this time something held me back.

She was pleading now. "Make love to me again, Oh God, please, Dean."

I arched an eyebrow and gave her a faint, knowing smile.

"A sixth time, Candy? Even I have my limits. All right," I sighed. "But first I have to pee."

[Six times? We know we're in the land of fantasy – no reflection on Mr. Opperman – the key element is exaggeration.]

She looked at me with wanton eyes. "What do you mean you have to peeeeeeeeeeeeeeeeeeeeeeeeeeeeeeeeeeeeeeeeeeeeeeeeeeeeeeee?"

Her voice was suddenly annoying, persistent, like a buzzer – like an alarm clock. The greatest lover in the world opened his eyes. *I was in another bedroom now. It was morning. God, I have to pee. What time is it? 7:32. Shit! It's Monday and I overslept! How did that happen? Oh, God, I'm late. I'm late! No, wait, it's Sunday. Oh God, I've really gotta pee. Where are my slippers? Why did I think it was Monday? What's wrong with my memory? I need to do something about my memory. Isn't there some memory pill? I need to start taking that, ahh...ahh...what's that stuff called? Ahh, Guh...Gr...Gringo?* **Ginkgo!** *That's it. I better write that down. As soon as I finish going to the bathroom, I'm going to write that down. God, I really have to go. It's more important to pee now.*

Where're my slippers? I swear to God they get up and walk around in the middle of the night. Okay. Bathroom light. Newsweek. John Glenn on the cover. How long has this issue been in here? Just what I want to see first thing in the morning – John Glenn. Toilet paper? Oh, God, I'm out of toilet paper! No, there's a package on the shelf up there. Why do they wrap everything in heavy plastic like it's going to Venus? You need to carry a god dammed sheetrock knife to get anything open anymore.

[The recognition factor. We have all struggled with the way things are wrapped. Then there's scented toilet paper! A setup for the next line.]

That's weird when you think about it. It's almost an oxymoron. I doubt John Glenn used scented toilet paper. Okay, you're done. Pull up your underwear. No, take them off. You might as well take a shower as long as you are in the bathroom. No, coffee first. Coffee first, then a shower. Make coffee. Go to the kitchen and make coffee. Coffee. Coffee. Make a pot of coffee. How about tea for a change? No, coffee. A hot cup of coffee. Where are the coffee filters? I always keep the coffee filters right in this cabinet. I bought a brand new box of coffee filters the other day. They were right here on this shelf and now they are gone!

Somebody stole my coffee filters! Who would do a thing like that? My landlord. Probably snuck in here and stole them while I was gone yesterday.

[The mind begins to imagine some pretty weird things. The nonhumorous solution would be that he can't find the filters and leave it at that.]

There's a law against that. How am I going to make coffee without a filter? I know! Use a napkin for a filter. Sure! Why not? A paper napkin would make a perfectly good coffee filter. Unless it's **scented like the toilet paper.**

[The second punch line.]

All right then, stick that napkin in the coffee maker and throw some coffee grounds on top. Not pretty, but it works! That's American ingenuity, by God! They didn't have Melitta coffee filters in the Old West. The pioneers would have used a napkin in their coffee machines probably. Coffee Filters of the Old West. Ha! That's funny. I better write that down. "I'm Roger Mudd, join us for Coffee Filters of the Old West, next on The History Channel."

Hey, that's got potential! Gee, I love it when I get a good idea first thing in the morning.

[Dean thinks this awful idea is good, and that is very funny. The fact is this wouldn't work unless the idea was really bad. If it were even half-way good, it would ruin the joke.]

It's going to be a great day, I can tell already! Nothing like a good idea to get the day started right. As soon as I get this coffee started I'm going to go write that down. Coffee Filters of the Old West. Okay, fill the coffee maker with water. That's it. Now turn it on and go write that down. Hurry up. Let's see, I need a pen. There's a pen on the desk. This desk is a mess. Here's a pencil. Oh, here are my slippers! Right here under the desk! There's one mystery solved. Must have left them down there last night. Now, what was I going to write down? Ahh...the pioneers didn't use coffee filters.... That's not funny. What was it that was funny? Cowboys didn't have coffee filters in the old days, they had...? Shit! I can't remember what that was now. Son of a bitch! Every time I think of something funny, I can't remember what it was later! It had something to do with coffee beans and covered wagons or something.

What's that sound? I hear raindrops. Is it raining? It's coming from the kitchen. Oh shit! I forgot to put the coffee pot under the coffee maker! Son of a bitch! There's hot coffee all over the drain board! Dammit! Where's a towel? I can't find a towel! Find a towel. Find a towel! Unplug the coffee maker. No, put the coffee pot under the coffee maker to catch the drips and then find a towel. There's scalding hot coffee all over the floor now! Find a towel. It's falling on the floor! I can't find anything when I need it around here! Use a napkin! Okay, just sop up the coffee and try not to get pissed off. It's too early to get pissed off. It's too early to be on your hands and knees mopping coffee off the floor with paper napkins, but that's not the point. The point is...?

I'm losing my mind. I really am. What's wrong with me?

You haven't eaten breakfast. That's what's wrong. Low blood sugar. Make breakfast. You need a healthy breakfast to get off to a good start. I'm really hungry. **Donuts!** *No, that's junk.* **Go get donuts!** *No.* **Yes!** *No.* **Donuts!** *No! NO MORE JUNK. You're eating*

Writing Humor

a healthy breakfast every day from now on. Starting right now.

What's in the fridge? Let's see here. Eggs. I could make an omelet. I could make a healthy omelet. I've got vegetables. Let's see. Pea pods. A pea pod omelet. Never heard of that. Squash. Cauliflower. A cauliflower and squash omelet. Nah. What's in the dairy drawer? Cheese. American cheese, cheddar cheese and coffee filters. **What the hell are the coffee filters doing in with the cheese?!** *Jesus, I really am losing my mind! I need coffee, that's why. I just can't think without coffee in the morning. Okay, start over. Just cool it and start over!* **Breathe....** *All right! Now, just start over and make a new pot of coffee.*

[What a wonderful way to find the coffee filters. The best element in humor writing is surprise. Dean names all the vegetables and then gets to the punch line.]

*Open the box of coffee filters and put one in the coffee maker. That's right. Now, put coffee in the filter. Not too much! Whoa. That's good. Now, put the pot under the coffee maker this time! Now turn it on. Was that hard? No. No big deal. I'm losing my mind. I really am. I've got to get some of those memory pills. Whatever they are. Starts with a G...Guh...Geh...***Ginseng!*** *That's it. Now go write it down right, now, before you forget. Where's that pencil? I just had it a minute ago! The pencil is in the sink. What's the pencil doing in the sink? Oh yeah, I dropped it when I ran in here to clean up the coffee. God, I'm a space case! Isn't that coffee done yet? It'll be noon before I get through screwing with this coffee machine. I could have walked to Starbucks and back by now. I spend a hundred dollars for a German coffee machine and it takes a week to make a cup. That's what I get for buying a German coffee machine. It's a Nazi machine. I have a*

Nazi coffee machine in my house. How lame is that? I didn't even want to buy this machine in the first place. I was hoodwinked by that beautiful blonde at Macy's. But she wanted me, I could tell. "I'll bet this machine would look great on your kitchen counter," she said. "Yes," I wanted to say, "and you'd look great standing there next to it every morning."

Leaning against the kitchen counter, the soft morning light from the bay window streams through her long blonde hair creating a halo of fire. Slowly the white terrycloth robe drops from her shoulders and falls to the floor. I arch an eyebrow and give her a faint, knowing smile.

"But Carla darling, I haven't even had my coffee yet."

"I know but I can't wait any longer," she says in a breathy voice. Reaching for the honey jar, she provocatively takes a spoonful and... What am I doing here with this spoon in my hand? Oh yeah, I'm going to use it to stir my coffee. Okay, it's almost ready.

Where's my favorite coffee cup? My red coffee cup. Where's my favorite coffee cup? I always leave it in the same place, right here in the rack. Now it's missing too! I swear to God somebody is playing with my head! Where is my good red coffee cup with the big handle? It was right here yesterday. Where did I have it last? In the car. I left it in the car yesterday. But I can't go out to the car because it's raining.

No, I thought it was raining, but it's not. Go get your coffee mug out of the car. Wait a minute, I'm naked. I have to put on clothes before I go outside. Oh, who cares? Just run out there nude and grab the cup out of the car. Screw the neighbors. Haven't they ever seen a naked man before? Just run down the driveway naked and grab the cup out of the car. It'll take five seconds. If anybody sees me, I'll just wave. Who cares what the neighbors think? I don't care what they think! Yes, I do. Put on some clothes. Wait a minute now, there's no sense putting on clothes before you take a shower. Take the shower first. Then put on clothes. No, wait. Coffee first. Then a shower. Then clothes. All right, slow down a minute. You better eat something first because you are not sane. A bagel. Heat up a bagel in the microwave while you decide what to do next.

Put the bagel in the microwave and set it at thirty seconds. Okay. Maybe if I run down the driveway nude, the woman in the house next door will run outside naked too and we'll make love on her lawn.

[The introduction to the fantasy.]

"Dean, oh, Dean! I've waited weeks. Love me now!"

I glance at her golden breasts then arch an eyebrow and give her a faint, knowing smile.

"But Daphne, darling, shouldn't we turn off the sprinklers first?" The early morning sun streams through the mist and a perfect rainbow envelopes the two of us. Daphne grabs my massive shoulders and pulls me closer.

"I don't care who sees us, Dean! I want the universe to know my passion for you. Take me!"

I kiss her so hard, I hear bells.

[The transition out of the fantasy.]

It's the microwave signaling my bagel is ready. WHAT ARE YOU THINKING? Her husband owns a gun shop! Oh, here's my good coffee cup! On top of the microwave. God, I'm losing my mind.

Where's the sweetener? I can't drink my coffee without the sweetener. Where'd I put the sweetener? Knowing me, it's probably in the laundry room next to the Tide. Oh, here it is. This sweetener is probably what's causing my memory loss. "60 Minutes" said Sweet and Lo is owned by the Mafia. Great. That's just great. I'm putting Mafia sweetener in coffee made in a Nazi machine. This whole planet is going to hell. Oh, this coffee is good. Finally. Nothing like that first cup of coffee. Yes. It's the best part of waking up. The best part of waking up is Folger's in your cup.

Now I've got their jingle memorized. Bastards. You can't get away from it. They're brainwashing me. I'm switching brands next can. I am not going to be brainwashed by their jingles. Besides, the best part of waking up is not Folger's in my cup. The best part of waking up is peeing.

[The setup.]

No, the first part of waking up is peeing.

[The punch line.]

The best part of waking up is...ahh.... All right, coffee is the best part of waking up, but I'm not going to buy Folger's anymore because they've drilled that goddam jingle into my brain. I'm going to buy the most obscure brand I can find next time. Chock Full o'Nuts.

Try that maybe. That's a weird name. Who would buy a product called Chock Full o'Nuts? Me. I'd buy that. I'd march proudly right up to the check out counter with that coffee and tell the checker that, yes, I buy weird coffee.

She'd pull her long red hair back from her face with one arm, revealing huge breasts and her name tag. With a smoldering

gaze she'd smile and say, "My name is Brandy and I'm off in an
hour."

And so it goes every morning. Actual elapsed time, five minutes.

The frantic pace is essential in a piece like this. Dean's mind segues from subject to subject in a mad, yet logical, way. The reality of the various objects gives credence to his fantasies. In fact, they are the stimuli.

The main ingredient in all of the work in this chapter is freedom. The writers are unfettered by the truth and allow themselves to fancify, exaggerate, and outright lie. If, in any of the aforementioned categories, you write a piece and tell it like it is, you are merely reporting. But, if you take each incident that happened and use it as a basis for a new reality, you have succeeded in creating a humorous piece – providing it's funny. The fact is, this is a method, and if you practice it enough, you can succeed.

There is a sub-category of nonfiction that I call "In Response To." A celebrity or a person in the public eye makes a statement and the writer creates a humorous reply to it. The original statement is usually fatuous, self-serving, accusatory, or stupid. It can be one or a combination of all these factors.

Here is one that hits many of those bases. Michael Ovitz, once the top super agent and dealmaker in Hollywood, gave an interview to *Vanity Fair*. In it he stated that a gay Mafia was largely responsible for engineering his downfall. Paul Rudnick, a brilliant writer and playwright, wrote a response in *The New Yorker*, and here are a couple of excerpts:

The Gay Mafia has its origins in ancient Greece, when Don Plato first remarked to a group of graceful youths, "I am so over Carthage."

The Gay Mafia is rumored to have important ties to Nancy Sinatra.

Gay Mafioso are particularly fond of the movie Scarface," but they think it's the life of Joan Rivers.*

So you see, satire doesn't necessarily have to close on Saturday night. Scour the paper and you'll see that someone, perhaps even a politician, has uttered something that invites your satirical response. These kinds of remarks are also grist for parody. Remember: Satire makes fun of the original without copying the style. Parody mimics the style broadly.

9

Sitcom

People who work sitting down make more money than people who work standing up. —OGDEN NASH

WITHOUT A DOUBT, writing a successful sitcom is one of the most difficult forms of writing. There are so many technical requirements that must be met, so many hands in the pot, and so many divergent reasons to rewrite that the sitcom writer better have nerves of Kryptonite and an ego to match. But before we get into the philosophical ramifications it may be fair to warn you that submissions of scripts to producers of sitcoms only go through recognized agents. There are rare exceptions to this, however: 1. The producer is your mother or father. 2. Your mother or father knows the producer. 3. You have incriminating photos of the producer.

I interviewed three very successful sitcom writer/producers for this chapter. To my mind the show the first two, Cheri Eichen and Bill Stienkellner, wrote and produced is one of the classic sitcoms of all time: "Cheers." Besides "Cheers," they wrote "The Jeffersons," "Facts of Life," and "Who's the Boss." Here are some of the things they told me:

The process of writing a script for a sitcom begins with the pitch. The pitch is an oral presentation of the story idea. It should be delivered with enthusiasm and be as complete as possible. You should be prepared to answer any questions about the story idea. You should have at least four or five pitches and be ready to answer questions about them. This way you have a better chance. A couple of your ideas may already be in the works by staff writers. More than a couple may not be right for the show. They also suggest that your stories involve a topic from your own life's experience rather than just a string of jokes tied together. There should be some dimension; some real human emotions tied to the humor. To put it simply, the characters are real people. These characters are not aware of their comic behavior. They play it for real. Let's say they like one of your ideas (they being the producers). You then go on to the four- or five-page outline. This is where you tell the story in the two-act structure and lay out as many jokes as possible. After meeting with the producers,

assuming they like it, and armed with their notes and suggestions, you are then asked to write the first draft.

The first draft should include a tease and a two-act structure.
OK. What's the tease? The tease is that brief scene that comes on
the screen before the show actually begins. It may or may not
have anything to do with the plot that follows. It's the attention-
getter that comes before the show's main title and its main purpose is to stop the viewer from changing the channel. You can
understand that the tease must be very provocative and funny.

Most shows utilize a two-act structure, although there have
been some shows that use a three-act structure. "Seinfeld" began
a style where the structure loosened so that certain plot points
emerged helter-skelter throughout the show. They used jokes the
same way, but the setup is introduced in act one. The punch line
came in the middle of act two. Instead of a tease and two acts,
"Seinfeld" could have fifteen or twenty short scenes, some only a
couple of lines long. [Author's note: To me it seemed the
shows that were about the show being about nothing –
explaining the show to NBC, etc. – were more convention-
ally plotted than their regular-type shows.]

But for now let's talk about the two-act structure. Act one:
The conflict or problem is introduced. Things get worse and the
act closes with a chaotic climax. Act two: Things get worse again,
no solution, then everything is resolved. Now hidden in that main
story is a B story, which may or not involve the main characters.
It too has a structure that follows the main story. Problem, problem, worse problem, then a solution.

The first draft is about forty-five to fifty pages long and it is
now or never for the writer. You must take your best shot. The

dialogue must be believable, the jokes as good as you can get them, and the structure, the problems and conflicts, credibly solved. Hopefully you will have captured the strengths and frailties of the characters. You now, as they say, "take" another meeting and thoroughly go over the first-draft script. Now one of three things can happen: 1. They decide it isn't working period and toss it. 2. They decide you have done what you can on the script and send it to their staff to rewrite. 3. They like your work and ask you to rewrite the second draft based on the notes from the meeting. (The producers can also send the script to their staff for their ideas. These, in turn, can come back to you to incorporate into the script.) The second draft is then polished, line by line, by the whole staff. It is now ready for the actors to read.

The actors sit at a long table with the director, the producers, and the writers. The moment of truth has arrived. As they read, the dreaded notes are taken. Once again, based on these notes, the appropriate rewrites are done. The new script is put on "its feet." That means the actors are now given the appropriate action by the director, e.g., stand on this line, move over there and then say your line, etc. This is called blocking for the camera. At this point it may become necessary to add a line or two due to the physical action on the set. You may have written, "Sure thing." But the actor has to walk fifteen feet to get to the next position. So in order to cover the walk the actor needs a couple more lines.

Other problems may creep in. The actor is having trouble with a couple of lines and can't make them "work." This necessitates another rewrite to accommodate the actor. Finally the producers, the actors, and the writer are reasonably satisfied the

Writing Humor

script is ready to shoot. Do you shoot it? No. There is one more run-through. This time there can be as many as twenty people watching and making notes.

Twenty new sets of notes. Twenty new opinions: good and bad. Twenty more reasons to do yet another rewrite. And who are these people? They are the NETWORK. They are the suits, the execs, the people who own the means by which your TV show reaches the millions of viewers.

Finally, and this is nearly the final finally, the show is run for a tech rehearsal. That is where the lighting and camera work are planned. After that, the audience is seated and the dress rehearsal is run for them. This is filmed as insurance in case something goes wrong when the actual show is run. After the dress rehearsal there may be some minor line changes – surprise laughs appear where least expected and expected laughs dissolve into silence – then the actual show is run before the live audience.

If you don't have an agent and you still want to write sitcoms after reading the previous pages, there are things you can do to achieve your goal. First you must watch the sitcoms you wish to write for. You must study the characters, take note of the writing style and the kinds of stories they use. I would pick at least four different shows. You may be able to download their scripts from the web. If you live in Los Angeles, the scripts are in the library of the TV academy. If you do get to read the scripts, you'll see that many times what's on the page is not on the screen. That's because the actors may ad lib a line here and there or there were last-minute changes on the shoot. You also have to be somewhat of a historian. You don't want to write a spec script (a script you write for no pay) about something they just did a few months ago. Test out the idea on friends. Imagine the sitcom characters saying the lines. Give each character an attitude no matter how small the part. Lillith, Dr. Crane's wife in "Cheers," was a part-time character until the writers fell in love with her portrayal. There have been many instances in sitcoms where one-time characters were so appealing they became regulars on the show. Don't try to create a whole new approach to the show. It's OK to take a regular character and write something fresh for him, but your spec script shouldn't reinvent the show.

After you've finished four to six spec scripts, you can query agents who represent writers for TV. Bill Steinkellner suggests you write shows that other writers like. "The Simpsons" and "Frasier" were two he mentioned. Undoubtedly you will be rejected time and time again, but if you persist, and your material is good, some agent will read it and take a chance. Another approach is to apply for a job as a production assistant on one of the shows. Get to know the people on the show, make friends. Watch how the show is put together and drop graceful hints that you aspire to be a comedy writer.

The following is the second act of a "Cheers" script written by Cheri Eichen and Bill Steinkellner. It's called "Thanksgiving Orphans." In the first act we learn that Diane is the only one who has actually been invited to a Thanksgiving dinner. And it isn't an ordinary dinner. It's at her professor's house and several literary celebrities will be there, including John Updike. In her usual uppity manner, she tells all who'll listen about the celebrities she'll meet. Sam, Carla, Norm, Cliff, and Frasier decide to have a dinner over at Carla's house. The end of act one shows Diane, dressed as a pilgrim, ringing Carla's doorbell. Carla opens the door and, as Diane says "gobble gobble," slams the door shut. It is important to note that act one ends with a sight gag (Diane in the ridiculous costume) and leaves the audience wondering what the devil Diane is up to. In other words, there is a laugh and a question that needs answering.

THANKSGIVING ORPHANS
by Cheri Eichen and Bill Steinkellner

INT. CARLA'S HOUSE.

THE DOORBELL RINGS. WE HEAR DIANE'S VOICE.

DIANE

Hello?

SAM

Come on, Carla, let her in.

SAM MOVES TOWARD THE DOOR. CARLA THROWS HER BODY IN FRONT OF IT.

CARLA

There's not enough turkey to go around.

SAM

We'll carve thin.

CARLA

Oh, all right. Maybe she'll choke on a drumstick.

[The ongoing feud between Carla and Diane always has Carla making sarcastic remarks about Diane's uppity manner and ineptitude.]

CARLA OPENS THE DOOR.

CARLA

What do you want?

DIANE

I'm afraid my golden afternoon turned to dross. The moment I entered the home of my professor I was greeted by a man with a clipboard who handed me a tray and told me to serve a daiquiri to Miss Radziwill. Can you believe it? We students were invited not as guests, but as domestic help!

[The clue here is the name Miss Radziwill, who at the time was constantly in society columns. Another comedic idea is that Diane, who earlier boasted about going to such a distinguished dinner as a guest, now finds out she was wrong. Also note that "her golden afternoon turned to dross."]

FRASIER

Diane, I really feel for you. Brought in under false pretenses and humiliated like that.

DIANE

Thank you, Frasier.

CLIFF

Did you tell the guy off?

DIANE

I dropped the tray, burst into tears, and fled.

[Fled? Most people would say "and left." Not Diane.]

FRASIER

Were I you, I'd call that professor and nail his sheepskin to
the wall.

DIANE

You're absolutely right.

DIANE GOES TO THE TELEPHONE AND BEGINS TO DIAL.

CARLA

Or better yet, march right back over there and do it in person.

OTHERS AD LIB AGREEMENT.

DIANE

Shh. (INTO PHONE) Professor Narsutis, this is Diane
Chambers. Yes, the one who fled. Well, listen Mister, I want
you to know that I'm appalled at your presumption and your
gross abuse of your station.... Well, for one thing I don't like

being mistaken for a waitress.

CARLA

No problem there.

[Carla has bitched at Sam since Diane came to work that she was a lousy waitress. Carla cannot let a thing go by.]

DIANE
(INTO PHONE; CHANGING HER TONE)
Really? (TO OTHERS) He's invited me back. They set up a folding chair for me at John Updike's table.

THE GANG AD LIBS "GREAT! YOU GOT TO GO!" ETC.

DIANE (CONT'D)
(INTO PHONE) I'm sorry sir, I can't. I'm here with my friends, my support system, and no matter what you offered, I don't.... Hello?

SHE HANGS UP.

[The fact is they hung up on her, but true to her character she puts a spin on it.]

SAM
You turned him down?

DIANE

Now that I find myself in the warmth of your company, how could I possibly leave?

EVERYONE AD LIBS "TAKE THE MASS AVENUE... TRY I 93" ETC.

DIANE

Oh you holiday hooligans!

CARLA

Oh-oh. Half-time's over.

ALL START TO GATHER BACK IN FRONT OF THE TV.

DIANE

(INCREDULOUS) You're watching sports?

CLIFF

Don't worry Diane, the game's almost over.

DIANE

I hope so.

ANGLE ON TV. WE SEE TWO TEAMS PLAYING.

DISSOLVE TO:

TELEVISION SCREEN – LATER.

WE SEE TWO DIFFERENT TEAMS PLAYING.

ANGLE ON LIVING ROOM. ALL THE GUYS ARE NOW SITTING ON THE COUCH WATCHING TELEVISION. DIANE IS IN THE MIDDLE LOOKING BORED. THE GUYS AD LIB "GO, GO!"

DIANE
Is this still the same game?

CLIFF
Overtime.

ANGLE ON TELEVISION. THE GAME CONTINUES.

DISSOLVE TO:

TELEVISION SCREEN – LATER.

EVEN DIFFERENT TEAMS ARE PLAYING. DIANE PASSES BEHIND THE GUYS ON THE COUCH.

DIANE
Isn't this game over yet?

NORM
Not yet.

DIANE

But their uniforms are different colors than before.

CLIFF

They change whenever someone scores a touchdown.

[This is a pretty tried-and-true sequence, and you'll notice it occurs three times (a magical number in comedy): The ignorant observer being fooled by the people in the know. Diane's questions are the straight lines. The jokes belong to Cliff and Norm. Next comes a switch, and the writers set up Diane's complaint and falsely bring her into the group by assuming she doesn't want to watch basketball, but would rather watch football.]

DISSOLVE TO:

CARLA'S LIVING ROOM NIGHT.

ANGLE ON TV SCREEN. WE SEE A BASKETBALL GAME IN PROGRESS. ANGLE ON DIANE PASSING THE COUCH.

DIANE

Now wait a minute.

CLIFF

Diane's right. Let's switch back to football.

NORM

Listen everybody, the guest of honor should be done in a few minutes. *I think it might be time we adjourned to the dining room.*

DIANE
Bravo, Norman. At least one other person realizes that this day is more than just an excuse to vegetate in front of a TV set, watching steroid-inflated savages bloody each other over a piece of pigskin.

DIANE MOVES TO TURN OFF THE TV. NORM STOPS HER.

[Not only is her assumption wrong, but notice her language and how she seeks an ally in Norm.]

NORM
Who said anything about turning off the TV?

NORM AND CLIFF PICK UP THE TV CONSOLE AND TURN IT TOWARD THE DINING ROOM.

CUT TO:

INT. CARLA'S DINING ROOM – CONTINUOUS.

THE GANG FILES IN.

CARLA
Okay, we'll be sitting boy-girl, boy-girl. Clavin you can sit anywhere.

SAM

(TO WENDY) [NOTE: Wendy is Sam's date. The usual gorgeous non-intellectual type.] *Save me a seat. I've got to see a man about a horse.*

SAM EXITS.

WENDY

(TO DIANE) *He isn't really going to see a man about a horse.*

[Pretty much a line that any of Sam's dates could say. Not PC, but the fact is there are dumb men and women in this world.]

DIANE

I'm so glad you're here.

[The sarcasm highlights Diane's disdain for Sam's taste.]

*WE HEAR A **DING** FROM THE KITCHEN.*

NORM

Oh boy, Tom Turkey on line one.

NORM EXITS. DIANE REACHES FOR THE WINE BOTTLE.

DIANE

Carla, may I do the honors?

AS CARLA EXITS TO THE KITCHEN.

                    CARLA
No, but you can pour the wine. And don't forget sponge cake.
(INDICATES WENDY)

                    DIANE
Of course not.

DIANE FILLS WENDY'S GLASS.

                    WENDY
Ooh, red. And I'm wearing red.

[Easy, but funny.]

WENDY DOWNS IT AS SAM ENTERS.

                    SAM
Diane, what is Wendy drinking?

                    DIANE
A cheap Bordeaux.

                    SAM
Wine? You gave Wendy wine?

                    DIANE
Yes. What's the matter?

SAM

She can't drink.

ANGLE ON WENDY POURING HERSELF ANOTHER GLASS
AND DOWNING IT.

DIANE

Oh. Oh dear, I'm sorry. Is Wendy...?

SAM

*Nah, nothing like that. It's just when she has a belt or two
things start to disappear...like her clothes.*

WENDY

*(UNBUTTONING) Is it getting warm in here or is it just
me?*

CLIFF

No, it's warm. Boiling.

[On the surface, a very innocent remark, but coming from
Cliff it has a dirty-old-man aspect and becomes a laugh.]

WENDY

(TO FRASIER) Hey, you're cute.

WENDY MOVES CLOSER TO FRASIER AND STARTS PLAY-
ING WITH HIS HAIR, THEN BEGINS SLIDING DOWN HIS
LAP, HEADING UNDER THE TABLE.

FRASIER

Oh my.

SAM

Wendy, come on up.

SAM PULLS WENDY OUT FROM UNDER THE TABLE.

WENDY

I'm tired.

[Setup for the joke, which is:]

FRASIER

The story of my life.

SAM LEADS HER OUT OF THE DINING ROOM. CARLA ENTERS FROM THE KITCHEN.

SAM

(TO WENDY) Come on, sweetheart, we'll let you take a nap in the other room.

CARLA

Don't let the baby bite her.

THEY EXIT. NORM ENTERS FROM THE KITCHEN.

NORM

Listen guys, the turkey's not quite brown yet.

CLIFF

What color is it?

NORM

Beige.

ALL MOAN.

[The pop-up thing is a setup for later.]

NORM

Don't worry. I turned up the gas and reset the timer. That little pop thing should pop any time now.

WOODY

I hope it hurries, I'm starved.

DIANE

Well, I suggest we make the most of this delay and engage in one of my family's favorite little Thanksgiving traditions.... Sam, I know you're standing in the hallway. Get in here.

SAM ENTERS.
SAM

Rats.

DIANE

In lieu of grace, we take turns standing up and toasting that for which we are thankful. Sam, since you're already standing,

Ian Bernard

you may begin.

SAM

Oh all right. I'm thankful I've got good friends, a good car, and nice threads.

DIANE

If you're going to make a mockery of this you may sit down. Frasier?

FRASIER

I'm thankful I know a guy who's got good friends, a good car, and nice threads.

DIANE

Thank you Frasier. Norman, why don't you share your blessings?

NORM
(TEARING HIMSELF AWAY FROM THE TV.)
I'm grateful that this game is tied at seventeen in the closing minutes of the fourth quarter so there'll be a fantastic finish.

DIANE SWITCHES OFF THE TV. DISGUSTED.

DIANE

I'm sorry you're all so short on gratitude. But I'll take up the cudgels, for I've many things for which to be thankful.

WE HEAR THE TIMER "DING" IN THE KITCHEN.

Writing Humor

NORM

Oh yeah, and I would like to give thanks for that turkey in the kitchen which needs to be checked.

HE EXITS.

[The next series of lines are very much like the earlier football sequence. They use the passage of time to build the humor. It once again shows Diane's pretentious sense of herself. She's also oblivious to the reaction of others: Her world is all that counts.]

DIANE

I'm thankful to be here today. I guess it was best said in the good book: for I was hungered and ye gave me food. Thirsty and ye gave me drink. A stranger and ye took me in…naked and ye clothed me.

CARLA

In self defense.

[Another zinger from Carla, who, as I said before, never lets anything go by. The writer's description of Diane (unfazed) shows Diane's isolation from reality. Again, there are three sections to the gag.]

DIANE

(UNFAZED) Sick and ye visited me…in prison and ye came unto me…

SAM BEGINS FILLING GLASSES AND THE OTHERS DRINK
AS WE:

TIME DISSOLVE:

INT. CARLA'S DINING ROOM.

SOME TIME LATER. THE WINE IS GONE. EVERYONE
LOOKS CRANKY AND BORED. DIANE IS STILL ON HER
FEET.

> DIANE
> ...huddled masses yearning to breath free. The wretched
> refuse of your teeming shore. Send these tempest tossed
> homeless to me. I left my lamp outside the golden door.

NORM ENTERS FROM THE KITCHEN.

> SAM
> Well?

> NORM
> Dark beige.

OTHERS GRUMBLE AS NORM EXITS INTO THE KITCHEN.

> DIANE
> Oh, don't be grumble heads. Besides, this gives me an oppor-
> tunity to toast a few special people who have influenced my

life so dearly. Teilhard De Chardin, Maude Gonne,
Caravaggio...

[The funny part is Diane believes this to be true. She isn't a
phony as much as she is completely deluded. The writer's
choice of names adds to the joke.]

NORM'S HAND EMERGES THROUGH THE SERVICE WIN-
DOW WITH A SIX PACK.

CARLA GRABS IT AND BEGINS DISTRIBUTING.

TIME DISSOLVE TO:

INT. CARLA'S DINING ROOM.

SOME TIME LATER. THE GUYS AND CARLA ARE SHRED-
DING NAPKINS, ROLLING SMASHED BEER CANS, AND
DOING OTHER THINGS TO DEMONSTRATE THEIR BORE-
DOM AND IRRITABILITY. DIANE CONTINUES TO THANK.

DIANE
Shari Lewis and Lambchop...

[After Caravaggio and De Chardin, the final joke is Shari
Lewis and Lambchop, who not only do not exist in the same
high-class world as the others, but were probably people
Diane watched on TV as a child.]

NORM ENTERS, LOOKING QUITE FRUSTRATED.

NORM

The little pop thing won't pop out. Something's wrong with it.
[The reappearance of the pop-up thing. This time with a payoff.]

CARLA

Maybe something's wrong with you.

NORM

No. It's definitely the little pop thing.

WOODY

Sometimes those little pop things can be really tricky. On the farm, turkeys are born without those little pop things.

FRASIER

The little pop thing has a name. It's called a thermometer! Can we all say the word "thermometer"?

NORM

We can say it until we're blue in the face, but it won't make it pop out any faster. I'm beginning to think it's a lost cause. I don't know about your oven, Carla.

CARLA

Hey, my oven was just fine before you stuffed Birdzilla in it.

SAM

Come on guys, let's not bite each other's heads off.

CLIFF

That may be all we get to eat today.

SAM

Give me a break. This other stuff looks fantastic. Who else wants some of these (TAKES A BITE) ice-cold potatoes?

CLIFF

They should be perfect with this body-temperature salad.

FRASIER

The crudities are nothing to write home about.

CARLA

Well, pass my peas. I made them, so I know they're okay.

NORM

Was that remark directed at me?

CARLA

No, it was directed at your stupid turkey and your stupid stuffing and your stupid gravy.

[The conflict is coming to a head. Because "Cheers" was a show that used character-based humor, it was certainly necessary to always have a certain amount of conflict. This propelled the plot, and because the characters all knew each other so well, they could, to put it colloquially, push the right buttons.]

NORM
What's wrong with my gravy?

CARLA
Nothing, except you could walk across the skin on top of it.

NORM
I'm sorry Julia Child. Here's your perfect peas.
(HANDS HER THE BOWL) Oops, spilled one.

NORM FLICKS THE PEA AT CARLA.

CARLA
Thanks. Hey, listen, I didn't mean what I said about your gravy. Look, it's fine.

SHE PICKS OFF THE SKIN AND FLICKS IT AT NORM. IT HITS CLIFF.

WOODY
May I have a roll, please?

CLIFF
Parker House or Pumpernickel?

HE THROWS TWO ROLLS AT WOODY.

WOODY

Parker House. Keep the Pumpernickel.
(THROWS THE ROLL BACK AT CLIFF)
And I don't need this butter, either.

WOODY THROWS THE STICK OF BUTTER AT CLIFF.
CLIFF REACHES FOR A HANDFUL OF SALAD. EVERYONE
BUT DIANE REACHES FOR FOOD IN SELF-DEFENSE.
DIANE STANDS, HORRIFIED.

DIANE

People! People! Stop this immediately. Never have I wit-
nessed such a silly sophomoric display of....

SAM LETS HER HAVE IT IN THE FACE WITH THE MASHED
POTATOES.

DIANE

Sam Malone, kiss your butt goodbye!

SHE BEGINS HURLING BREADSTICKS AT SAM.

CARLA

FOOD FIGHT!

EVERYONE BEGINS HURLING FOOD. NORM HEADS TO
THE KITCHEN.

[At this point it matters little what anyone says. Here are all the characters we know so well having a great time throwing food, and like the ancient pie-in-the face routine, it is funny.]

                         NORM
             (OFF STAGE) Hey! It's ready!

EVERYONE FREEZES. NORM ENTERS CARRYING A
BEAUTIFULLY DONE TURKEY.

ALL OOH AND AAH.

                         DIANE
             Oh, it's beautiful.

                         NORM
             Let the Thanksgiving begin.

NORM SETS THE TURKEY DOWN ON THE TABLE
REVEALING ONE-HALF OF A BEAUTIFUL ROAST TURKEY
AND THE OTHER HALF, A PICKED-AT CARCASS.
EVERYONE GIVES NORM AN ICY LOOK.

[A sight gag, plain and simple.]

                         NORM
             I had to test it.

                                        CUT TO BLACK.

> CLIFF (IN THE DARK)
> Sam, could you pass the cranberries?

> SAM
> They're on your forehead.

END OF ACT TWO

The jokes all emanate from our familiarity with the characters. Except for the cliché bimbo gags, none of the dialogue goes out of the way to just make a joke. But even the bimbo jokes are in character as we know that Sam Malone boasts that he prefers that kind of date. Would it be funny if Wendy were a normal woman, with average intelligence? Cheers longevity owed so much to the audience's relating to and believing the characters. So many sitcoms rely. too heavily on jokes and fail to build this character/audience rapport. That is probably the most singular reason for their failure.

My second interview was with Jennifer Crittenden. Jennifer began her career as an intern for David Letterman. She was lucky in that she became Mr. Letterman's personal intern. Her duties were to "cut pineapple slices, fetch coffee, and Xerox." After a while she asked permission from the producer to submit jokes for the opening monologue, and the producer would take some of them to David Letterman. If any of them were accepted they paid her $100 a joke. I might add that Jennifer was on summer vacation from college, so when the summer was over she went back to school. But during that brief stay on the Letterman show she met an agent who encouraged her to get in touch after she graduated.

She did just that and moved to Los Angeles. On the agent's advice, Jennifer began to write spec scripts for various shows. "It's best," she said, "to write for a different show other than the one you submit to. That way you avoid comparison with their team of writers, who obviously know the show so well that your script would not stand up to their standards."

After a year of writing scripts for various shows and sending them to her agent for comment, Jennifer got into a young writers program at Fox – unfortunately this doesn't exist any longer – and went to shows and observed. She then asked if she could pitch a story idea to "The Simpsons" production. They liked the idea and put her on staff, where she stayed for two years. From there she pitched some ideas to the "Seinfeld" team. They bought four stories, but none of them were produced. But they did like her work enough to hire her as a writer – the only woman on staff – and she stayed for two seasons.

Which brings us to "Everybody Loves Raymond," where she worked as a writer and co-producer. Before I go into the "Raymond" show procedure, I must comment that Jennifer's career path seems very smooth. But I should point out there was a lot of dedicated work and a purpose to her method. The lucky break was to be the kind of intern who had access to David Letterman, and Jennifer took advantage of that. Now to the "Raymond" show:

The executive producer prefers the writers to pitch ideas that emanate from their own life's experience. If the pitch is acceptable, they will then write what they call a two pager (more often a three to four pager). The two pager is a beat-by-beat outline of the story, making note of the ending for act one and the ultimate payoff in act two. The two pager is discussed with the other writers and either goes on to be written as a script or is rewritten as a two pager. The two pager also goes to the executive producer, Ray Milano, the star of the show, and then to the network. They also send back notes which will affect whether or not it proceeds to the script stage.

"Everybody Loves Raymond" is primarily a one-plot show: that is, unlike "Seinfeld," which usually had four different story lines, "Raymond" sets up a premise and follows that premise to the conclusion. Let's say the two pager is approved by all and the writer now submits the first-draft script. It's important to note that the two pager on "Raymond" lays out a very strong structure, one that is seldom changed, so that the subsequent drafts of the script concentrate on joke revisions.

Jennifer remarked that on "Seinfeld" they would throw out whole story lines, which would necessitate massive rewrites that would go on into the early AM. "And sometimes," she said, "they would do the deed during the shoot, so they had to rewrite while the audience waited."

Back to "Raymond": *The first draft is then shown to some of the other writers and they give notes. It is then presented to all of the writers and the show runner (the executive producer) and* hopefully all they do is improve the jokes. The script is then sent out to the actors for the next day's table read. This is where the actors sit around a table and read the script. The writers hover on the periphery and take notes: which jokes worked, etc. The network representative is also there, and she hands her notes to the executive producer. The rewrite, based on the reading, takes place that afternoon.

The next day they do a run-through and then another run-through for the network executives. The process is always being tweaked and jokes improved. "Everybody Loves Raymond" only shoots one show. The audience sees it for that first-time shooting. If they need to, they will shoot inserts or pickups. This is where the camera goes in close just for a particular line or two. And quite often that line is changed, making a new joke, which elicits a fresh response from the audience. "Raymond" is an ensemble-type show, and the scenes tend to be long. Whereas a show like "Seinfeld" could have twenty scenes, "Raymond" will have four. But there is one common denominator for all sitcoms. Act one must end with a big laugh and leave the audience wondering how the story will end. The methodology of the "Raymond" show makes for a saner atmosphere than most shows. This is due partly because the show uses children and there are strict rules about how long they can work. But I think the main reason is the show producers make strong decisions at the two-pager stage, thus eliminating a lot of uncertainty as the script progresses. Most writers will agree that changing dialogue is much easier than changing structure. When you meddle with the basic architecture of the piece, it can become a house of cards and you might have to start all over.

"Raymond" shoots about three or four minutes over the

required twenty-two minutes. This makes the edit so much easier. "Seinfeld," for instance, would shoot six or seven minutes over the allotted time, which made for difficult decisions in the edit room. One last thing: The "Raymond" scripts average about forty pages.

On a recent show, Larry Gelbart, the veteran comedy writer of so many TV shows, movies, and stage plays, commented: "Try not to write so every character sounds like a comedy writer." Which takes us back to an earlier comment. Character. Character. Character. Successful sitcom writing is based on credible characters, albeit a little over the top, making funny comments. It is not about everyday, ordinary people doing everyday, ordinary things. It is not about nutty wise asses who make jokes about everything and lead a cartoon existence. If you study the most successful shows you will see that the jokes define the character. And it is the audience's sense of recognition that makes the lines funnier.

There is one other vital ingredient to the sitcom and that is physical humor. It can be as slight as a raising of an eyebrow or it can be as broad as pulling a chair out from someone. Even "Fraiser," one of the more cerebral shows, has ventured into slapstick. There was a long scene with Niles where he decided to iron his pants and he set the couch on fire. Not a word was spoken and the scene lasted at least four or five minutes. The writing of a good scene utilizing physical humor must go into explicit detail for each action. You can be sure that a good actor will enhance this by adding her own touches, but all the visual clues should be on the page.

10

Interviews

THESE FOUR INTERVIEWS OFFER DIFFERENT PERSPECTIVES on writing and the business of writing. John Cleese is both a performer and a writer. "Fawlty Towers" is one of the most popular TV shows of all time. He also wrote *A Fish Called Wanda,* a hugely successful movie.

Fannie Flagg began her career as an actress. I first met Fannie at the Santa Barbara Writer's Conference, where she began work on her book *Fried Green Tomatoes at the Whistle Stop Café.* Her latest book is called *Standing in the Rainbow.*

Larry Gelbart began his career in television. Along with Neil Simon, Woody Allen, and Mel Brooks, he wrote sketch comedy for Sid Caesar. He also wrote the M*A*S*H movie and the Broadway hit *A Funny Thing Happened To Me On The Way To The Forum.*

Marta Kauffman came from writing shows in New York to television. She is a most successful writer/producer with shows such as "The Jeffersons" and the current hit "Friends."

JOHN CLEESE:

IAN: *When did you first discover you had a humorous bent?*

JOHN: *I think I was about sixteen. I started doing what we call house entertainments. I was in house with some sixty boys at school and I remember doing these skits and being enthused by it in a way that only soccer and cricket enthused me up till then. I loved the idea of working with a group. I remember doing a funny Hitler impersonation as the movie* The Great Dictator *was playing then. After I graduated I went off to teach English history and geography for two years and didn't do anything theatrical. When I got to Cambridge I joined the Footlights almost by accident, through a friend. I wrote a couple of sketches, very derivative, but they worked and I got hooked by it. In 1963 the Footlight show was transferred to the West End (England's Broadway), and I had written quite a lot of that show. A couple of people noticed that, and BBC signed me up. At that point I was going to become a producer/writer. I was perfectly happy with that as I didn't consider myself a performer. And so my mind set was that I was a writer. If it were not for the fact that a writer gets paid so much less than an actor, I probably would have done more writing.*

IAN: *How do you get the idea to the page?*

JOHN: *In the early stages you get a bunch of ideas but you really don't develop them. They don't have any legs. As you get better you try to work on ideas that can be developed. That is they can*

Writing Humor

generate new things from the original idea. This eliminates the one-joke kind of sketch where after the joke nothing happens. When you recognize the ability to go beyond the one joke, you don't waste your time working on a piece that doesn't go anywhere.

IAN: When you write, do you know it's going to be funny?

JOHN: I don't think you ever really know whether it will be funny. William Goldman said, "Nobody knows." Even in a successful show you are apt to misjudge a scene. In A Fish Called Wanda, the scene where I speak Russian was doubled in length after we played it for some people, and the scene where Michael Palin chokes on the apple was cut in half because the audience got upset with his discomfort. So you never know if it's funny or just how funny. All you can do is get a decent percentage.

IAN: What about the process?

JOHN: I found you don't need a tremendous amount of creativity, but rather a good sense of logic. Very frequently people think comedy is about having a lot of ideas. I think it's more to do with having a smaller amount of good ideas and then tying them together in a logical framework. For example, in Wanda I knew early on that I had the beginning and end. The big problem was what happened in the middle. I think that comedy is so hard to write that you have to get an ending before you write anything else. I knew what was happening to my character and Jamie Lee Curtis's character, and I was trying to construct parallel stories with Kevin and Michael. I realized that Kevin on his own wasn't as funny as when he was with Jamie Lee. So instead of writing Kevin solo scenes I integrated him into my involvement with Jamie Lee. Then I wondered what does Michael do during that time? I asked myself what would he be doing? It then came to me that he was a great pal of George so why wouldn't he be trying to eliminate the one witness against George? He tries to kill the old lady, but he doesn't succeed. Now I've established that Michael is an animal-lover. And if in trying to kill the old woman, instead he kills one of her pets, that would be very funny. Funny only because of Michael's love for animals and the horror he feels when he accidentally kills one.

This illustrates that not only can conflict between characters be funny, but conflict within the character can be very funny. That is when one layer of the his personality fights against another layer. To young writers: Don't always look for new ideas from the outside. Try to find all of the things that could happen to your characters within a narrower area. Look at all the possibilities of behavior with the characters you have already written. If you stick with that you can often tease out new ideas that are inherent in the material you already have. That always feels more integrated and makes better comedy than constantly putting in new ideas, introducing new characters or new concepts.

A FISH CALLED WANDA

I wrote thirteen drafts of Wanda. Five of them were fairly major rewrites. It took about a year. I rewrote my character, making him much more realistic. It wasn't as much fun to play, but it worked for the story. We also shot the ending three times before we got it right. I usually start with the plot. I don't bother to write any dialogue until I have the structure clearly in mind. The idea that the structure will fall into place while you're working on character and dialogue seems to me terribly unrealistic. The way I like to work is to figure out the plot as accurately as I can, e.g., "Fawlty Towers." Connie Booth (the co-writer who also played the hotel maid) and I would take up to six weeks to write one episode, which is about four times as long as people usually take to write a half-hour show. And we didn't bother to write any dialogue for two weeks. Now if we thought of a funny line, we'd put it down. We used to do a hundred and thirty-five pages for one half-hour episode. We'd have four hundred camera cuts instead of two hundred. There's so much in them, so they do allow repeat viewing. You'll see different things each time you watch the show.

Back to the script: No matter how much planning you do there is always the possibility that something will need changing. Pascal said that fortune favors the prepared mind. And that's true. The more prepared you are the more things tend to fall into place. I progressed from writing short sketches to half-hour shows then to movies. Of course the more difficult writing job is when you extend the time to a full-length movie, which is usually about two hours long. People can't laugh for that length of time. The fact is, they don't want to. The audience needs time to breath, and the writer has the responsibility to keep them interested. You might make them laugh thirty or forty minutes and that's enough. But those in-between places have to have a plot and character so you care about the people and care what happens. William Goldman once gave me a bit of advice and I would recommend it to new writers. Go to a movie and see it three consecutive times. By the third time you are no longer emotionally involved and you are able to analyze what the writer did. You can also notice when people leave to go to the restrooms. Why did that moment in the movie lose them? With sketches, I used to listen to one I had done, then try to rewrite it from memory. I'd do this once again and listen to it performed. By doing this I could begin to see why certain lines had to be in a different order. One of the advantages of putting a sitcom in a familiar place is that people know what is to be expected. A lot of comedy is about disappointing expectations.

So you set something in a hotel and they know how a person at the desk is supposed to behave, and when that person acts as Basil Fawlty does, it becomes quite funny. Whereas if you set the location let's say in a funeral parlor, you have to teach the audience the norm of the place, as it is unfamiliar to most and that makes the humor much more difficult. You want to know what's the norm as soon as possible so you can break with it and fool the audience. I would have liked to write mysteries. I think Hitchcock had four or five set pieces and then stitched them together in a logical way. In comedy I'm looking for four or five scenes that I think will be exceptionally funny. Then I determine where they will go in the movie and I space them so they occur at the right time. Again, with me, it's a matter of logic. If this happens to A because B does something, then what is the consequence of that action. If you follow that pattern throughout the movie, you should be creating a cohesive structure. I also examine what my various characters are doing for the length of the movie. Are they interesting whenever they appear? Earlier I referred to Michael Palin's role in Wanda and how we concocted the sub plot of his wanting to kill the witness. It is important that all of the ingredients make sense and hopefully add to the fabric of the movie.

There's no reason to believe that you have to write in one particular style. I have always been drawn to farce and the manic energy of farce. But even there you have to begin with a setup. You can't be funny until the setup is complete. No matter what kind of comedic piece though, it is important to keep it at one level: consistent in tone, e.g., if a farce gets wilder and more broad, you can't come back to being sensible again.

FANNIE FLAGG:

IAN: How do you develop what you are going to do?

FANNIE: I just think about things that haunt me. What interests me are ordinary, middle-class people. I find them to be not only endearing but also hilariously funny, but they don't know it. They all have their little idiosyncrasies. Sometimes I'll start with a line such as, "I don't honey, as hats go, I've seen worse." And I'll just use that as the opening line of the scene and develop it from there.

I use little bits and pieces, things that I hear and see. I take a lot of notes on characters and write a lot of names down in situations. "Well I killed the Griggs boy," one of my characters says. This old lady gets mad at this little boy who's throwing rocks at her cat, so she puts Ex Lax in some fudge. She means for him to have just one piece, but he eats the whole plate so she thinks she's killed him. It starts with the line and develops into a scene or two.

I don't base the character on real people but rather on a character type. I love little old ladies for some reason, they just crack me up. They say funny things and the way they think is very funny.

IAN: The chapters that begin with a piece of dialogue then have to meld into the book. How do you do that?

FANNIE: I will get very quiet...relax, and all of a sudden the characters will start talking to me. And I can hear them. It's almost like I'm a secretary just taking down what they say. Then the scenes go off in different directions that I haven't even thought of. I seldom rewrite. I've learned to trust my initial instincts, but of course there are times when they are wrong or need modifications. Most of the time, if I listen real carefully, they say the things they're supposed to say.

IAN: Do you worry about structure?

FANNIE: Well it does worry me at times, but there's not a lot I can do about it. You know I could write for forty-five years without thinking of a plot. I think basically what I am is a short-story writer but I smash it all together to make it a novel. As you know I write short chapters. The characters create a plot. Not me. The things they do and the actions they take create the plot. Many times I will write about characters and the things they've done (things I didn't know before) and all of sudden it becomes part of the plot. When you listen to the characters as I do, they take you to all sorts of places you never dreamed of. I suppose if I thought of plot first, my characters may well refuse to follow. I don't want to be stuck in that position.

IAN: Are you conscious about making the characters grow or change, becoming better or worse?

Fannie: I like to introduce a character then gradually drop things in about them so you find out more and more as the book goes on. It's very much like real life. The longer you know someone, the deeper the friendship grows and you get to know more and more about them. The most fascinating thing about people is you meet someone and you're talking to them and all of a sudden you find out the most amazing things about them. And a lot of the time the most fascinating ones won't say a thing about themselves, but someone else reveals the information. I was in Alabama doing an appearance for the governor. My mother came with me, and we were assigned a highway patrolman. He was about six four, very matter of fact and tough looking. And I thought, boy this guy is probably the meanest, roughest guy that ever lived. He drove us for three or four days, and my mother, who's very friendly, asked him how he got to be on this special governor's honor guard. I was expecting him to say, "Well, I killed forty-five people" or "I arrested a huge dope ring," etc. He looked in the mirror and said, "The truth is I have sort of a little problem. So many young people got killed on the highway and I had to go tell their parents. I just broke down. I couldn't bear to do it anymore. So they pulled me off that duty and put me here." And I thought, Wow! did I misjudge this man. Because of his appearance I thought in clichéd terms, and after he spoke I realized that who he was, was deeper than what I thought. The physical picture had nothing to do with who he was.

I also think the environment plays a part or has an influence on characters. You see them in one place and they're quite ordinary; you put them someplace else and they shine. I write the things I know most about. The middle-class world...ordinary folk. I'm most comfortable with them. Just do what you do best.

IAN: Do you add characters as you go along?

FANNIE: If they want to be in the book they let me know it. I start a book and I have no idea this person is going to be in the book. For instance, in this book I'm writing now a man shows up and he's the funeral king. His logo says "I don't want your business but I'm here when you need it."

I do a lot of research. This time I'm writing about white gospel, so I read every book that's ever been written about it. I listen to the music and go hear it. I need to know that everything

I write about it is true. I must be totally convinced that I know all I need to know about the subject I'm writing about. I find if you're authentic, it's hard to make mistakes in the writing of the characters. When I began writing for "Candid Camera," I found there is nothing funnier than the truth. When I read a book, I'm particular about the writer portraying the characters in the social level where they live and giving them dialogue that truly belongs to that class. You have to stay true to the language, their level of education, their habits, attitudes, the food they eat, and the way they dress. If you do that right you can be sure the things they do will be quite funny. But you must treat them with respect and dignity. In other words, you don't have to make fun of them because they are funny enough just being natural. Sometimes I go out to bowling alleys and talk to people. Or small coffee shops where the early birds, the regulars, come in, and we talk about the news or whatever.

One of the reasons I write is I can control time. It's something we can't do in real life. So in my books I go back and forth in time. Once you have established a character strongly enough I feel you can flip back and forth in time and the reader will follow. I'm interested in how my characters got to be that way, and you can indicate that by showing them twenty years earlier, for instance. Everyone has a history behind them, and I think it interesting to show bits and pieces of that as the book goes on.

I read this in a newspaper article and it set me wild. All it said was a woman drove up to the steps of the county courthouse, rolled down the window, and threw her mother's head at somebody. She shouted, "Here, this is what you wanted." Then she backed the car up and drove away. Well it made me wonder what the heck had happened to get to this act. What made her so frustrated that she chopped her mother's head off and threw it at the courthouse.

You have to write with a point of view. You just can't report things because they happened. You have to develop a very strong voice of your own. And you can make comment, if you're careful, and the reader won't even notice.

One of things I have to watch out for is not to have my own agenda. A lot of writers put their own agenda in a book and it doesn't work. What you have to do is get out of the way. My advice to writers is to get out of the way and just let it come. People who write humor are very serious about a lot of things, and they have to be careful not to take themselves seriously. You should always try to keep it light. Then when you need to do a scene that calls for a serious touch it is much more effective.

IAN: OK. You have all of these vignettes or short chapters. How do you put them together?

FANNIE: Now I want you to understand that I am not advising all writers to do this. It happens to work for me, and please don't laugh. I take the chapters and hang them on a clothesline in the hall. Then when I think I'm through I go down the line and put them in order. It helps if you have a long hallway. That can also be a huge disadvantage. I look for a beginning, a middle, and an end. You see, I don't write in a linear way. I write all around the book and in some way it gives me more freedom. One of the difficulties is you never know when you're through. You can stack most of the chapters and still be left with a few hanging in the hall. On Fried Green Tomatoes, I wrote six endings. To this day I hope I chose the right one.

I struggle very hard to write, it doesn't come easy. I find it very difficult to go into a room by myself and write, but I have a sign over my desk that reads "It's not cancer, it's just a book."

LARRY GELBART:

IAN: Was there ever a project that went through several rewrites, with different assorted people offering suggestions and "help"?

LARRY: Way back in the sixties there was a play called Fair Game, by Sam Locke. It was a slight play and it starred Sam Levene. It was about a woman who got a divorce and was working for Sam in his Seventh Avenue garment company. Because she was a divorcee, she was considered fair game. It ran 187 performances simply because people loved Sam Levene. Then it was bought for the movies by Charlie Feldman (a very famous agent and producer). He hired me to write the screenplay, but he had an aversion to Jewish characters. He said two things to me, "I don't want it to be Seventh Avenue" and "I don't want it to be a Jewish guy." He asked me to come up with an alternative idea. He was going to use William Holden in the Sam Levene part. So I turned the draft in and he said it wasn't that good but it didn't matter as he had a whole new take on the story. He wanted me to do another draft because he'd signed Jeanne Moreau. So Sam Levene, then William Holden, suddenly became a French woman. Suffice it to say, I didn't write the next draft.

Later I was working at CBS and they hired Nat Hiken, the comedy writer, to just hang out with Phil Silvers. They went to ball games, to delis, they played cards…the idea was that Phil could have a series tailor-made for him. My office was next to the executive producer for Phil's project, and one day he pointed to a

Writing Humor

cardboard box on the floor. "Do you believe it," he said. "A year of spending CBS's money and all they could come up with was a G.D. army show?" The show was "Sergeant Bilko," and of course as soon as it became a hit, it was all his idea.

There was another great switch by an actor later on. I pitched an idea to Dick Shawn about a sabra, an Israeli who came over to sell bonds. He ended up in the garment district, and when he saw how the gangsters were controlling the business, he was going to teach the Jews to be tough and take care of the mobsters. Well I drove to New Jersey to pitch the idea to Shawn and he loved it. When I got back to New York his agent called and said Dick loved the idea, but would it possible, instead of an Israeli, could the hero be an Eskimo. As I hung up the phone I somehow had the feeling this project wasn't going anywhere.

IAN: Did you ever do extensive rewrites and end up with what you started with in the first place?

LARRY: Forum [A Funny Thing Happened on the Way to the Forum]. We spent five years writing ten separate drafts, all very difficult to do, and then we were lucky enough to get George Abbot to come on board. He asked us to thin out the plot because as written an audience would never follow it. We made the condition that we could put something back in if we felt it needed to be there. So after thinning, weeding, etc., we ended up with the book we had before all the difficult and tedious rewrites. You know, it goes this way: You write the first draft for yourself and from then on you write draft after draft to please other people.

IAN: This can be a royal pain in the posterior, can't it?

LARRY: Yes!

MARTA KAUFFMAN:

Ian: When did you first discover that you wanted to write?

Marta: I still haven't discovered that. OK, sometime during college, some twenty-five years ago, my partner, David Crane, and I met and we were acting at the time. We started talking about doing a show together and he said let's write something that we can be in. We then discovered that it was more fun to do that than act, so we just began to write a bunch of things. We wrote what everybody writes in college – a college musical called Waiting for the Feeling. *I'm still waiting. Well as you know, David and I co-created "Friends," and it all began twenty-five years ago.*

Ian: How did you go from college to becoming a professional?

Marta: I graduated a year before David and moved to New York, still thinking I might be an actress. But every weekend I went to Boston because David and I were writing another musical. It was called Personals, *and it was based on the personal ads in the paper. In 1980 we went on a USO tour with the show and we performed all over Italy and Germany. After that the show was produced off Broadway in 1985. An agent who saw it asked us if we might be interested in writing for television. By the way, to this day she's still our agent.*

[Author's note: To keep a partner and an agent for twenty-five years is a feat seldom seen in show biz.]

Ian: So what was the first show you wrote?

Marta: David's father was an announcer for a television station in Philadelphia, and he did a cable show called "The Knowledge Bowl" and we wrote the questions. Then we did an episode of a show called "Everything's Relative," with Jason Alexander.

He was in our musical Personals, so he got us in. We were so excited, so we wrote it and then went to the first run-through. They left in one line of ours and rewrote everything else.

IAN: What was the line?

MARTA: "I think it's his appendix."

IAN: I remember that line.

MARTA: Yes. It's a classic. After that we decided to come to L.A. The people at ICM (a large talent agency) said we'll get you on staff somewhere. We said no. We don't want to be on staff, we want to do our own show. One of the producers we met on that trip had a lot of footage of 1950's television shows, and he asked us what we'd do with that footage. We said we would think about it, and we did, and that became "Dream On". We wrote the pilot, but we didn't think it would become a series so we continued to look for work. We then got a job with Norman Lear, writing pilots. Norman didn't love us. We were in the company kitchen one day after handing in a script and Norman walked in. I tried to hide behind the refrigerator, but he saw me, came over and took my hand, and said, "It's very shallow." Then he went to David and said, "Superficial." So for years I was shallow and David was superficial. Then "Dream On" went on HBO. That was when we met our third partner, Kevin Bright. He was producing the show. So they put us in a tiny room and we began to write the show. About that time, Norman Lear came back and told us he wanted us to write a pilot. We were both very surprised. David said, "He hates us, so let's write a show he'll never make." We were told no politics even though the star of the show was a senator. The wife was a maid-slapping lesbian. The daughter was bulimic. The son-in-law was suicidal, and in the pilot he tried to hang himself. So we were now sure they'd never ever do this show. They did it. And they did it for two seasons. By the way it was called "Powers That Be."

IAN: *Did that set you up as a creator of shows?*

MARTA: *Actually, "Dream On" did. After that we made a deal with Warner Brothers and one of the pilots we did over there was "Family Album." We learned a very valuable lesson about this time. That is: Don't write anything unless it comes from your heart. For instance, they wanted us to write a "white collar" Roseanne. Now that makes sense, doesn't it? Anyway, we tried and the show didn't do very well. We were then asked to write a high-school comedy, which we did. The network said it was too young and they wanted it to be more adult. Of course if we had written an "adult" high-school comedy, they would have thought us inept. At the same time we wrote the script for "Friends."*

IAN: *Was that immediately accepted?*

MARTA: *Yeah.*

IAN: *Could you describe the steps from idea to production?*

Marta: *In television, first you have your studio. They give you notes like, "How do we know it's her birthday?" And you say, "There's a big sign that says Happy Birthday! There's cake and candles, etc." And then you have your network. They're kind of the boss, especially when you're doing a pilot. One of my favorite experiences on "Friends" – I'm a feminist – was when Don Olmeyer was running NBC. Feminist and Mr. Olmeyer, not too good. In the pilot episode, Monica sleeps with a guy whose story was that he hadn't been able to do this for three years. So when Don says, "She deserves what she gets," the fire starts coming out of my nose and my partner David was gesturing for me to calm* down in the corner. Well, Mr. Olmeyer had a questionnaire made out for the audience with questions like: For sleeping with a guy on the first date is Monica (A) A whore? (B) A tramp? (C) Easy? But the lesson we learned from this was a way to listen to the network's ridiculous demands. In this case, we made the guy someone she had cared about for a long time and that made her more sympathetic. Generally we are much harder on ourselves than they will ever be on us.

IAN: How many people make notes on a "Friends" script before it is shot?

MARTA: I believe it's a gazillion. My favorite place to get notes is from Standards and Practice. They're the people who tell you what you can or cannot say and what you can or cannot do. We had an episode where Monica and Rachel were fighting over the last condom. Now we thought this was extremely responsible television. No one's having sex unless there is a condom. That's a good lesson. So we're told you cannot ever show the condom wrapper. Now just a year ago a "Seinfeld" show showed a close-up of a condom wrapper. But that's the kind of thing we deal with each week.

IAN: How many writers are assigned to the show?

MARTA: This year we have fourteen, including me and David.

IAN: How are ideas generated for the show?

Marta: A lot of times we sit around after the weekend and we all talk about what happened to us. Then it strikes us that one of the stories would be great for Phoebe, or Joey, or whomever. Usually we break up into two groups. One group will be working on the stories we need. The other will be working on the rewrite on the current script. Mainly we throw ideas around and we laugh a lot. You have to be willing to be pretty frank about your life and problems. Out of this may come three stories that then go up on a board. Then we have to work out the time and location situation. With a large ensemble cast, we have to make sure that so and so can be at the park at that time. In other words, the characters must be in a logical place so the audience believes it. We also have to think about a certain parity for each character. That is, we can't have ten Joey stories and just two Phoebes. Then we do what we call an ABCing of an idea…that is, going over it scene by scene. The show is constructed with a tease, act one, act two, and then a tag. This outline is then given to a writer who goes off to write a first draft.

IAN: How long does that first draft take the writer?

MARTA: Beginning of the season, two weeks. End of season, four days. In the beginning of the season they get to do a second draft. We give notes and they go away for a few days. Then the whole group reads it and everybody writes notes. All of our big discussions are as a large group. These are smart, funny people and they are hired because of that. So we want to hear what they have to say. Then we break up into two groups again, and the original writer is in with the group that will do the rewrite. Then we go through every word, every line. When that is done, that is what we call the table draft. That is what the actors read at the table. Based on how the actors read it, we then do a rewrite. Then we do the first run-through for just the producers and writers. Then, based on that, we may do another rewrite. Then the network and studio come to see a run-through and they make their notes. This entails another rewrite. On Thursday we do a camera blocking rehearsal and I take two writers with me to that. If necessary we do some rewriting there on the spot. Friday we do a camera refresh, and then we do it in front of an audience, and then, you guessed it, another rewrite. We only shoot the show once, but if a scene doesn't work we'll shoot it three or four times. We also do pickups – close-ups where they can change a line as often as they like because the audience is no longer there.

IAN: I lost track of how many drafts there are.

MARTA: Seven drafts. Scripts average between thirty-five and thirty-nine pages.

IAN: How many stories are there in one show?

MARTA: Always three. One main story with the bulk of the pages and the emotional center and two lesser stories. The B story is a little lighter and the C story is a runner…something silly. The C story will usually involve the characters who have little to do with the A story. As you can see, the process is complex and difficult, but we do have fun. If something doesn't work, we try to fix it. And if the fix doesn't work, we throw it out and begin again. The satisfaction is hearing the audience laugh at a line, get sad when they're supposed to, and in general, really enjoy the show.

11

Accept Rejection

IN A RECENT ARTICLE, Flannery O'Conner stated that as a girl she read the humorous works of Edgar Allan Poe. I had never thought of Mr. Poe as a humorous writer, so I went to the library to search for his funny stuff. Well, Miss O'Conner was right. For there, in a volume of complete works, were several very funny stories. The excerpt I chose is from a story called "The Literary Life of Thingum Bob, Esq." In the story, Mr. Thingum imagines himself a poet and sends poems to a few magazines. I should mention he steals the poems from various sources and signs them with the name Oppeldeldoc. The following are the letters of rejection. You'll soon see they are far more personal and to the point than our modern-day ones, which always thank us for our efforts, BUT...etc., etc.

"THINGUM BOB, ESQ."

by Edgar Allan Poe

Oppeldeldoc (whoever he is) has sent us a long tirade concerning a bedlamite whom he styles "Ugolino," who had a great many children that should have all been whipped and sent to bed without their suppers. The whole affair is exceedingly tame – not to say flat. Oppeldeldoc (whoever he is) is entirely devoid of imagination.... Oppeldeldoc (whoever he is) has the audacity to demand of us, for this twaddle, a "speedy insertion and prompt pay." We can neither insert nor purchase any stuff of the sort.

Another reply:

We have received a most singular and insolent communication from a person (whoever he is) signing himself "Oppeldeldoc." Accompanying the letter of Oppeldeldoc (whoever he is) we find sundry lines of most disgusting and unmeaning rant about "angels and ministers of grace." As for this trash, we are modestly requested to "pay promptly." No sir! No!

And finally:

A wretched poetaster, who signs himself "Oppeldeldoc," is silly enough to fancy that we will print and pay for a medley of incoherent and ungrammatical bombast which he has transmitted to us.... We have half a mind to punish this young scribbler for his egotism by really publishing his effusion as he has written it. We could inflict no punishment so severe, and we would inflict it but for the boredom which we would cause our readers in so doing.

The nice thing about rejection is it has no favorites. No matter how many books a famous author has written, there is always the possibility of rejection. I think we would all be

Writing Humor

surprised by the number of times certain famous short-story writers for such prestigious publications as *The New Yorker* had serious fights with editors over rejection. The fact is, rejection can mean different things: 1. The work is no good. 2. The work needs work. 3. The work doesn't appeal to the editor for obscure professional and personal reasons. 4. It doesn't matter how many people reject the work, the next person may love it. It was rumored that *A Confederacy Of Dunces* was rejected by many, many publishers and was published after John Kennedy Toole's death due to the persistence of his mother and the assistance of Walker Percy. The history of publishing is full of such tales. So if you think rejection is the end of your career, you are wrong.

THE WORDS YOU WRITE ARE BUT A SMALL PART OF YOU. THEY CAN BE REARRANGED, REPLACED, AND EVEN ELIMINATED...BUT **YOU** REMAIN THE SAME. THE GOAL OF REWRITING AND EDITING IS TO MAKE THINGS BETTER, SO TRY NOT TO BE OFFENDED WHEN SOMEONE SUGGESTS YOU DO THAT. LIKE THE GODFATHER SAID, "IT ISN'T PERSONAL."

The following comforting thoughts are by Steve Martin from a recent *New Yorker*:

Writing is the most easy, pain-free and happy way to pass the time of all the arts. As I write this, for example, I am sitting comfortably in my rose garden and typing on my new computer. Each rose represents a story, so I'm never at a loss for what to type....

It is true that sometimes agony visits the head of a writer. At these moments, I stop writing and relax with a cup of coffee at my favorite restaurant, knowing that words can be changed, rethought, fiddled with and ultimately denied. Painters don't have that luxury. If they go to a coffee shop, their paint dries into a hard mass.

Remember: There's never been a funny painter.

Aldous Huxley once wrote: "A bad book is as much a labor to write as a good one." So please, out of respect for the two weeks it took me to write this one, be kind.

Acknowledgments

"A Paris to Strasbourg Flight" by Ernest Hemingway. Fawcett Publications and Byline Ernest Hemingway, Inc.

Florida Straits by Laurence Shames. Dell.

Shaw on Music. Doubleday Anchor.

Stormy Weather by Carl Hiaasen. Alfred Knopf.

High Fidelity by Nick Hornsby. Berkley Publishing Group.

Get Shorty by Elmore Leonard. Dell.

Decline and Fall by Evelyn Waugh. Penguin.

Dave Barry's Greatest Hits: Why Humor is Funny by Dave Barry. Ballantine.

Catch 22 by Joseph Heller. Dell.

Something Happened by Joseph Heller. Alfred Knopf.

Small World by David Lodge. McMillan and Warner.

"Tea at Mrs. Armsby's" from *The Owl In the Attic* by James Thurber. The Universal Library, Grosset and Dunlap.

Without Feathers by Woody Allen. Warner Random House.

"At The Funeral" by Mark Twain. Harper and Rowe.

The Rising Gorge by S.J. Perelman. Simon and Schuster.

Pnin by Vladimir Nabokov. Vintage Books, Random House.

Notes From a Small Island by Bill Bryson. Avon Books.

Lake Wobegone Days by Garrison Keillor. Viking.

"Across the Street and Into the Grill" by E.B. White. *The New Yorker.*

Fried Green Tomatoes at the Whistle Stop Café by Fannie Flagg. Random House.

"Frank Lloyd Wright Meets Oscar Madison" by Barry Freidman. *Los Angeles Times.*

Practical Demon Keeping by Christopher Moore. Saint Martin's Paperbacks.

Antic Hay by Aldous Huxley. Random House.

"What Brings You to Our Fair Land" by Martin Amis. *The New Yorker.*

"Tooth Prints on a Corn Dog" by Mark Leyner. Random House Value.

Wonder Boys by Michael Chabon. Picador.

Dave Barry's Greatest Hits by Dave Barry. Ballantine.

Cheers script: "Thanksgiving Orphans" by Cheri Eichen and Bill Steinkellner. Permission by Viacom Consumer Products.

"Writing is Ease" by Steve Martin. *The New Yorker.*

With Special Thanks to:
Linda Stewart-Oaten
Dean Opperman
Shawn McMurray
Ernie Witham

IAN BERNARD has been active in music for fifty years. He has conducted and played piano for Rosemary Clooney, Dick Haymes, Vic Damone, June Christy, and many others. He was music director of the hit show "Laugh In" and has recently conducted and arranged an album for Michael Feinstein called "The MGM Album." On tour with Mr. Feinstein, Ian conducted the San Francisco Symphony, the National Symphony at Wolf Trap, and the Denver Symphony.

Ian also plays jazz piano and has worked with many great stars of jazz, including Shelley Manne, Chet Baker, and Art Pepper.

He is also a screenplay writer and author. His book *Film and Television Acting* has been in print for five years. South Coast Repertory produced his play *Chocolates*, which was also produced in New York.

He lives in Santa Ynez, California, with his wife of thirty years, Penny, who trains show horses. He has two children and four grandkids.

FANNIE FLAGG has had many successful careers, from Broadway star (*The Best Little Whorehouse in Texas*) to movie and TV actress (*Five Easy Pieces*, "Candid Camera," "Love American Style") to screenwriter and author (*Fried Green Tomatoes at the Whistle Stop Café* and, her latest, *Standing in the Rainbow*). Her first novel, *Daisy Fay and the Miracle Man*, was on *The New York Times* best-seller list for ten weeks, *Fried Green Tomatoes* for thirty-six weeks.

Ms. Flagg makes her home in Alabama and Santa Barbara, California.

CAPRA PRESS was founded in 1969 by the late Noel Young. Among its authors have been Henry Miller, Ross Macdonald, Margaret Millar, Edward Abbey, Anais Nin, Raymond Carver, Ray Bradbury, and Lawrence Durrell. It is in this tradition that we present the new Capra Press: literary and mystery fiction, lifestyle and city books. Contact us. We welcome your comments.

815 De La Vina Street, Santa Barbara, CA 93101
805-892-2722; www.caprapress.com